Pharaohs and Foot Soldiers

ONE HUNDRED ANCIENT EGYPTIAN JOBS YOU MIGHT HAVE DESIRED OR DREADED

by Kristin Butcher

art by Martha Newbigging

annick press

toronto + new york + vancouver

We acknowledge the support of the Canada Council for the Arts, the Ontario Arts Council, and the Government of Canada through
the Book Publishing Industry Development Program (BPIDP) for our publishing activities.

ONTARIO ARTS COUNCIL
CONSEIL DES ARTS DE L'ONTARIO

Cataloging in Publication

Butcher, Kristin
    Pharaohs and foot soldiers : one hundred ancient Egyptian jobs you might have desired or dreaded / by Kristin Butcher ; art by
Martha Newbigging.

Includes bibliographical references and index.
For ages 9-12.
ISBN 978-1-55451-170-9 (pbk.).—ISBN 978-1-55451-171-6 (bound)

    1. Occupations—Egypt—Juvenile literature. 2. Job descriptions—Egypt—Juvenile literature. 3. Egypt—Civilization—To 332
B.C.—Juvenile literature. I. Newbigging, Martha II. Title.

HD8786.B88 2009   j331.700932'09014   C2008-907033-X

Distributed in Canada by:
Firefly Books Ltd.
66 Leek Crescent
Richmond Hill, ON
L4B 1H1

Published in the U.S.A. by Annick Press (U.S.) Ltd.
Distributed in the U.S.A. by:
Firefly Books (U.S.) Inc.
P.O. Box 1338
Ellicott Station
Buffalo, NY 14205

Printed in China.

Visit us at: www.annickpress.com
Visit Kristin Butcher at: www.kristinbutcher.com
Visit Martha Newbigging at: www.marthanewbigging.com

For Hunter, Cole, and especially Brock—
because of the pictures.
        —K.B.

For Debbie and Cynthia.
        —M.N.

CONTENTS

INTRODUCTION

This book is about ancient Egypt and the sorts of jobs you might have worked at if you lived there. Egypt is located in Africa. That's the huge continent shaped like a horse's head. On the right side of it, beside the horse's ear, is the Red Sea. Follow the Red Sea up until you bump into land. That's Egypt.

Most of Egypt is desert. It is rocky, and sandy, and very hot. The only place people can live is along the Nile River, which runs right through the middle of Egypt. The Nile is the longest river in the world. It starts at Lake Victoria, in central Africa, and flows north into the Mediterranean Sea. As it passes through Egypt it turns the nearby desert into a green valley. Because of this, people say Egypt is *the gift of the Nile.*

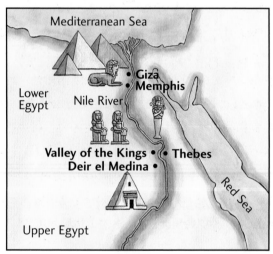

Today the Nile provides water, electricity, transportation, and soil for farming as well as beautiful scenery. If you took a boat ride up the Nile, you'd pass many bustling cities.

That's all very fine, but this book isn't about modern Egypt. It's about *ancient* Egypt, the time of pyramids and pharaohs (far-rows). It's about Egypt the way it was 5,000 years ago! That's not as long ago as dinosaurs, but it is still so far in the past that it's almost impossible to imagine. Of course there were no computers, telephones, or cars back then, but for quite a while ancient Egyptians didn't know what a wheel was either, and they'd never even seen horses!

That didn't stop them from building an amazing civilization that lasted 3,000 years. The best part is that they left mountains of evidence (well, pyramids of evidence, actually) of that entire time. This book is going to explore some of that evidence—the monuments, the tombs, the treasures, and the jobs. Especially the jobs.

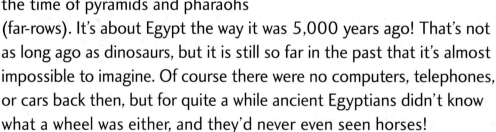

A TIME OF CHANGE—OR NOT

You would think that when ancient Egypt ended, it was a lot different than when it started. After all, 3,000 years is a long time. Things change. But the truth is things *didn't* change—at least not very much. That's because the Egyptians liked Egypt just the way it was. If it's not broken, don't fix it—that might have been their motto. Being surrounded by desert had a lot to do with the situation too. It wasn't easy traveling across all that sand and rock to visit other places, so unless they were traders or soldiers, most Egyptians stayed home.

Therefore they had no idea that while they were putting down roots along the Nile, another civilization was doing the same thing along the Indus River in India. They also didn't know that as they were building pyramids for their dead kings, the Mayans on the Yucatan Peninsula in Mezo-America were building pyramids too. Egypt bordered the Mediterranean, yet everyday Egyptians didn't really know much about the other civilizations that shared the sea. They never visited the Hanging Gardens of Babylon or saw a Greek play performed in an open-air theatre. For most Egyptians, life in Egypt was all they knew, and they were fine with that.

BC AND AD

Since nobody knows when time began, historians have set up a timeline using the birth of Jesus Christ as the starting point. Everything that happened before Christ's birth is indicated with the abbreviation BC, which stands for *before Christ*. Everything that happened after Christ's birth is indicated with the abbreviation, AD, which stands for *Anno Domini*. That's Latin for *in the year of the Lord*. So if Columbus sailed the ocean blue in 1492, he sailed 1,492 years after Christ was born, or in 1492 AD. Julius Caesar died 44 years *before* Christ was born, so we say he died in 44 BC. Look at the timeline below. Notice how the BC years count backwards. The bigger the number, the longer ago the year. So, though Julius Caesar was assassinated in 44 BC, he was still alive in 45 BC. Pretty tricky, isn't it?

... 10 9 8 7 6 5 4 3 2 1 <—BC   0   AD—> 1 2 3 4 5 6 7 8 9 10 ...

TIMELINE

3100 BC – Upper and Lower Egypt are united by Narmer—also known as Menes (Mee-neez). This event marks the beginning of ancient Egypt. Narmer became the first pharaoh, and Memphis (not the one in Tennesee) became the first capital city. Much later, the capital was moved to Thebes, and Memphis crumbled into ruins. The remains of it are very near the modern city of Cairo.

2685 BC – the building of the first pyramid. When ancient Egypt first began, pharaohs and wealthy people were buried in tombs called *mastabas*—(after they died, of course). *Mastabas* were made of mud bricks and looked like flat boxes with slanted walls. But then a pharaoh named Djoser (Zo-zer) came along and had a tomb built in the shape of a pyramid. The pyramid's walls looked like giant steps and the top of the pyramid was flat. The most important thing about this Step Pyramid was that it was made of stone. That's why it's still standing today.

3100BC	3000 BC		2685 BC	2000 BC

3000 BC (or thereabouts) – the invention of paper made from papyrus. The ancient Egyptians learned how to take the papyrus reeds that grew on the banks of the Nile River and turn them into a strong paper, which was rolled into scrolls. This was an important discovery. It meant the Egyptians could keep written records of everything they did. These records have helped us learn a lot about ancient Egypt.

2000 BC – the discovery of bronze. Ancient Egyptians were good at working with metal. They made beautiful jewelry and decorations from gold and silver, and they made tools and weapons from copper. Though copper was easy to shape, it wasn't very hard. Then one day someone discovered that if copper and tin were mixed together, a new, stronger metal was created. The new metal was bronze.

1665 BC – Hyksos (Hik-sos) invade Egypt. Though there weren't many visitors to ancient Egypt, there were some. The Hyksos were an Asiatic people who came from the eastern shores of the Mediterranean and used their superior weapons (like the horse and chariot) to defeat the Egyptian army. The Hyksos stayed in Egypt for less than 100 years, but that was long enough for the Egyptians to learn all about horses and chariots.

1365 – 1346 BC – lifetime of King Tutankhamen (Too-tank-ah-men). Everyone has heard of King Tut. He was only eight years old when he became Pharaoh, so adults known as regents ruled for him. In his whole life Tut never did anything worth remembering. But considering he was only 18 when he died, that wasn't really his fault. Tut is well known because of his tomb. When the archaeologist Howard Carter discovered Tut's tomb in 1923, it was exactly the same as it was the day Tut was buried. The tomb's seal had never been broken.

| 1665 BC | 1365 – 1346 BC |
| 1550 BC | 30 BC |

1550 BC (give or take a couple of hundred years) – the invention of the *shaduf* (sha-doof). In Egypt it hardly ever rains, so ancient farmers had to find other ways to water their fields. The *shaduf* was a great help. Made of a bucket on the end of a long rope attached to a swivel pole, the *shaduf* let farmers scoop water from the Nile, swivel around, and dump it into the canals and ditches that ran around their fields.

The Beginning of the End
30 BC – Rome conquers Egypt. Throughout the 3,000 years that ancient Egypt existed, it was invaded from time to time, but it always managed to hold together until the uninvited guests went home. But when the Romans came, things changed. Egyptian culture started to fall apart. Christianity and Islam replaced the Egyptian belief in many gods. There were no more pharaohs. The language changed too. So did the writing, and 400 hundred years after the Romans showed up, hieroglyphic writing was lost.

RED LAND/BLACK LAND

Egypt's geography and climate affected not only where people lived but also how they lived.

For four months every year, melting snow and heavy rains in the highlands of central Africa caused the Nile to flood its banks, leaving behind rich, black soil. So this is where ancient Egyptians settled. During the flood season, known as *Ahket*, it was impossible to work the land, so farmers served in the army or helped build temples and pyramids instead. Once the flood season was over, it was time to plant and tend the crops. The Egyptians called this season *Peret*. After that came *Shemu*. This was the drought season when the crops were harvested, tools were repaired, and irrigation ditches and canals were cleaned up.

Beyond the black land was desert. Because of its color, Egyptians called it the red land. Though the only Egyptians living in the red land were the soldiers who ran the army outposts, the desert was still important. Its extreme heat and endless sand made it difficult to cross, and therefore it was a good shield for keeping foreigners away. But the desert was also a source of gems, silver, and gold, as well as limestone, sandstone, and granite. The ancient Egyptians crafted the gems into jewelry, the metals into tools and weapons, and they used the rock to build pyramids and temples.

SOCIETY

Ancient Egyptian society was arranged in a sort of pyramid (Surprise!) with the powerful, rich people at the top and the poor people at the bottom. Obviously there were a lot more poor Egyptians than rich ones.

At the very top of the pyramid was Pharaoh. There were a few women pharaohs, but mostly they were men. Pharaoh was the king. To ancient Egyptians, he was also a god, so naturally he had the most wealth and power. Right below Pharaoh were the nobles, government officials, and priests, who were also well off. Next came the army officers and scribes. (Scribes were the guys who wrote everything down.) Life was pretty comfortable for them too. In the middle of the pyramid were the merchants and craftspeople. They had to work hard but were still able to earn a decent living. Farmers were near the bottom of the pyramid. Though they worked from morning to night to feed all of Egypt, they didn't get much reward. But they were still a step above servants and slaves—they were at the very bottom of the pyramid and had the hardest jobs. They worked for Pharaoh and other rich people at anything from quarrying stone and mucking out a stable to serving food. (After washing up, of course.)

Since children were usually trained to take on their parents' jobs, the pyramid more or less stayed the same for 3,000 years. A scribe might become a priest. A slave might buy his freedom. A successful craftsperson might become a merchant. A farmer might sell himself into slavery to pay off his debts. A priestess might become a doctor. But this bit of shuffling didn't change the pyramid.

ONE FOR ALL

Every culture has people who are old, sick, or disabled. Ancient Egypt was no exception. In other civilizations of the time, the only way these people could survive was to beg. Not in Egypt. Egyptians felt it was their responsibility to care for the less fortunate and integrate them into society. A mentally disabled man might learn to be a washerman. A blind man might become a musician. An old woman might sell vegetables at the market. An orphaned child would be adopted.

GODS AND GOVERNMENT

The ancient Egyptians had over 2,000 gods! Egyptians believed that at one time the gods had been alive and ruled Egypt. So naturally Egyptians wanted to stay in the gods' good books. Pharaoh was thought to be the only living god left, and he spoke for all the gods, which meant his word was law. He was the leader of the gods and the government.

But Pharaoh was just one person—even if he was a god—and he couldn't run Egypt all by himself. So he had other people do some of the work. He got priests to look after the temples, and he got noble-men called *nomarchs* (no-marks) to govern the different regions or *nomes* of Egypt. The *nomarchs* had to run things the way Pharaoh wanted, but they still had a lot of power, so they didn't mind. Pharaoh was also in charge of keeping Egypt safe, so he arranged for help there too. He appointed a Commander-in-Chief, who worked with three other commanders to organize a huge army.

The truth is that everybody worked for Pharaoh. Egyptian citizens had to perform a corvée (kor-vay), which was a sort of labor tax. Once a year they left their regular jobs—for most people this was during the flood season—and went to work for Pharaoh. They dug canals, worked in the mines, made roads, hauled building stones, and soldiered with the army. The only people who got out of corvée duty were the nobles and scribes.

SOME IMPORTANT GODS AND GODDESSES
Many of the Egyptian gods were
part human and part animal.

Re or **Ra**

Horus

Anubis

Isis

Thoth

Amun

Hathor

Osiris

Seth

Ptah

Re or **Ra**—sun god; most important god; has the head of a hawk with a sun disk on top

Amun—creator god; was often considered King of the Gods; most often shown as a man

Horus—sky god; Egyptians believed he was the living Pharaoh; has a hawk's head

Hathor—wife of Horus; goddess of women; shown as a woman with cow horns and a sun disk on her head

Anubis—god of embalming; he guarded the burial place; has the head of a dog or jackal

Osiris—god of the dead and ruler of the underworld; usually shown as a mummy with a white cone headdress

Isis—sister and wife of Osiris and mother of Horus; thought to be the mother of all pharaohs; shown as a woman with a throne-shaped headdress

Seth—brother of Osiris and Isis; god of violence and destruction; he is considered evil; has the head of an unknown animal

Thoth—god of writing and counting; god of wisdom; has an ibis head

Ptah (Ta)—patron of all craftspeople; shown as a mummy holding a staff

BELIEF IN THE AFTERLIFE

Ka

Life in ancient Egypt might seem like it was pretty tough, but compared to other civilizations of the time, Egyptians lived very well. They just didn't live very long. Getting old was so rare that Egyptians thought old people were magical—that they had been favored by the gods. But whether a person lived a long or short time, Egyptians believed that death was only temporary—a kind of waiting room between this life and the next one. Once people were buried, they came back to life.

Of course, it was a bit more complicated than that. The dead person had to cross a dangerous river, get past snakes and monsters, and then be judged by the gods. To make the journey into the next life easier, the families of the dead placed charms, clothes, food, and other everyday items in their graves.

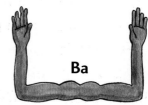

Ba

Egyptians believed that a person was made up of many parts, including the personality or life force, called the *ka* and the spirit or soul, called the *ba*. When a person died, the *ba* left the body, but once the burial was complete the *ba* went looking for its body again. That's why embalming dead people (turning them into mummies) was so important. It preserved the body, which the dead person was going to need in the next life. Embalming also made it easier for the *ba* to recognize itself when it went looking for its body.

If everything went well, the dead people went on to lives like the ones they had had before. (Not great news for slaves!) But if the dead people were found to be undeserving, they would be thrown to the Eater of the Dead. (Not a good choice either!) Only pharaohs got to go on and live with the gods.

BOOK OF THE DEAD
When people died, a scroll of prayers, magic spells, and instructions called the Book of the Dead was placed in their coffins to help them on their journey through the afterlife.

SHOW ME THE MONEY ...
I MEAN THE BREAD

There was no money in ancient Egypt. It's not that people were poor; they just didn't have money. Oh, all right—some people were poor, but even rich people didn't have money. Nobody did. Not even Pharaoh. Egyptians didn't use it. They measured wealth in land, cattle, fine homes, jewelry, the number of servants people had, the quality of their clothes, the food they ate, and how fancy a funeral they gave their parents.

That doesn't mean Egyptians worked for free. They got paid for their work and the goods they sold—just not in money. Egypt operated on a barter system. In other words, people traded for the things they needed—a goat for a basket of vegetables, a necklace for a stool, a bundle of papyrus reeds for a haircut.

The barter system was based on a copper weight called a *deben*. Everything had a value in *debens*. A pot might be worth 5 *debens* and an amulet (lucky charm) might be worth 10 *debens*, so if a potter wanted to buy an amulet, he knew it was going to cost him 2 pots. It may seem a bit complicated, but the Egyptians were used to it.

Pleasure doing business with you.

As always, sister.

One thing Egyptians couldn't live without was grain—wheat and barley, to be exact. People didn't go a single day without eating bread and drinking beer, and both of those things were made from grain. So people were often paid in grain. Pharaoh kept huge storehouses brimming with grain just so he could pay all his workers.

CHOOSING AN ANCIENT EGYPTIAN CAREER

Ancient Egyptians didn't have a lot of job choices. There were a lot of jobs—just not a lot of choices. Jobs were usually inherited, so children learned job skills from their parents: farmers' sons became farmers, sculptors' sons became sculptors, and so on. Nobles had a bit more opportunity. Depending on how well they got along with Pharaoh, they could land all kinds of important government jobs.

Women worked too, but they had even fewer choices than men did. It didn't matter if they were rich or poor, their number one job was having children and looking after the home.

Ancient Egyptians might not have been able to choose their careers, but you can. Imagine you could travel back in time and try out any of the jobs in this book. Would you want to be a tomb painter? How about a professional mourner? A dancer? A wrestler? If you like excitement, a charioteer might be the job for you. Do you like to be in charge? Then you could be Pharaoh!

Read on to find out!

CHAPTER 1

Army Jobs

At first Egypt had no regular army. Soldiers were conscripted as needed. But after the Hyksos invasion, in 1665 BC, Pharaoh decided a full-time fighting force was necessary. He built an army of over 100,000 soldiers—spear-men, axe and club men, slingers, archers, swordsmen, and charioteers. There were career soldiers, mercenaries (paid soldiers from other countries), and soldiers forced into the army against their will. But the army wasn't just soldiers. It also had cooks who prepared food, servants who waited on the officers, doctors who treated wounds and sickness, and scribes who recorded the battles. There were spies and scouts too.

The army's most exciting and important job was fighting wars, of course, but it did a lot more than that. Its troops provided escorts for mining expeditions and trading ventures. Soldiers guarded the temples and quarried stone for the tombs.

The army was highly organized. Pharaoh was in charge, but he had so many other jobs to do that he left the day-to-day army decisions up to his commanders. But whenever there was a battle brewing, Pharaoh put on his blue war crown and climbed into the nearest chariot.

Other countries didn't like fighting the Egyptian army—probably because they usually lost to it. And losing meant they might have a hand cut off so they could never fight again. A good fighter might be given the choice to lose a hand or become a soldier in Egypt's army. (Tough choice.) If Pharaoh was in a good mood, he might just order the prisoners be taken as slaves.

Soldiering was a hard life. There were endless marches through the hot desert and beatings for those who stepped out of line. Of every four soldiers wounded on the battlefield, one died. But for the men who lived and stuck it out, there were rewards: gold *flies of valour badges* for bravery, promotions for loyal service, and gifts of land and animals at retirement. Slaves who served in the army were often granted their freedom.

Archer

CAREER SOLDIERS

There were two kinds of career soldiers in the Egyptian army. Mercenaries were professional soldiers who hired themselves out to fight even though they weren't Egyptian. There were many mercenaries from other countries in Egypt's army. Then there were the career officers—nobles who were rewarded grandly for loyal service in the army. Pharaoh showed his appreciation with gold, land, and other honors. However, if officers' sons didn't follow in their fathers' footsteps and become soldiers too, Pharaoh took the gifts back.

BROTHERS IN ARMS

When on the march, soldiers traveled in groups of 10 to share camp duties and food. For training purposes they were joined by four other groups of ten to form a squad called a Fifty. During battles they united with three more Fifties to form a company or regiment. Each 200-man company fought with one kind of weapon and had a name and a standard or banner to identify it. One company might consist of archers, another might be slingers, another swordsmen, and so on. Companies came together to form divisions. These were the largest fighting groups, numbering 5,000 soldiers. Each division was named after a god.

You are an archer in the Egyptian army. You and the other soldiers in your unit rain arrows into the enemy lines to cause confusion and create a gap. This allows your army's chariots and foot soldiers to charge in. As the battle heats up, you try to shoot the horses of enemy chariots. The good part about your job is that you can do it from a distance. In fact, you can hit a target 400 m (1312 feet) away. In the Egyptian army, each fighting unit flies flags and banners. These help keep the troops organized, but they also show you which way the wind is blowing, so you can adjust your aim.

You use a powerful bow. Because it is made in layers, it is called a composite bow. The first layer is a long, curved strip of flexible wood. This is covered with bark, animal sinew, and horn. The bowstring is sinew too. You must be very strong to pull it. You wear bone guards on your fingers so the string won't cut you and leather bands on your wrists so your arms don't get scraped when the string springs back into place. You carry a quiver of 30 arrows. Some are made of wood, some from reeds. They are fletched with three feathers. Early arrowheads were made of stone or bone, but yours are bronze. They have different shapes. The thin pointed ones plunge deeply into your enemy. If they hit the lungs or heart, your victim will die quickly. The hooked arrowheads tear your victims' flesh wide open. This could be a slower death.

Someday you would like to be a chariot archer. Only the fiercest warriors achieve this rank. You stand in the chariot, beside the driver, with two quivers of arrows and a dozen small spears, which you use on enemy soldiers trying to flee.

Charioteer

Though you are a fairly young nobleman, you are one of the most important soldiers in the Egyptian army. You drive a chariot, and chariots are vital to victory in war. There may be as many as 500 of them charging around a battlefield—even more if you count the chariots the other army has. It takes a lot of skill to do your job. Though your chariot is light in weight—two men can easily carry it—it still takes a great deal of strength to control it, especially when you are traveling at breakneck speeds over rocky ground—and even bumpier bodies. (Trampling enemy soldiers under your wheels is part of your job.)

Your chariot is pulled by two horses, and the three of you work as a team. The horses are as highly trained as you are. You drive standing up with an archer beside you. Driving at full speed, you aim your chariot at the enemy troops. At the last second you change direction, so that the archer can shoot his bow or throw a spear. At such close range, he doesn't miss. The horses' hooves and the chariot wheels spit up stones and dust, and with a little luck, the enemy ranks break down and a hole opens in their lines. That is the cue for your foot soldiers to charge in with their swords and axes. If your archer becomes wounded or is killed, it is up to you to drive *and* fight.

If you like excitement and can drive a chariot, this is the job for you.

Foot Soldier

If you are a foot soldier in the Egyptian army, it probably wasn't your idea. You may have been put in the army to fulfill your annual corvée to Pharaoh, or—if the number of soldiers was down—you may have been conscripted (forced to join) by one of Pharaoh's scribes. Army life might be all right for officers, but for a simple foot soldier like you, it is very hard. Your only pay is the food you are given and the hope that you might share in the spoils of war. Sometimes you don't even get beer to drink.

A big part of army life is the long treks through the desert. Officers expect you to cover 24 km (15 miles) a day. You march side by side in columns with the merciless sun beating on your head. To make matters worse, you are loaded down with provisions. Your kit weighs around 27 kg (60 pounds). Water is hard to come by— after all, you *are* in the desert—and your 9 l (2.5 gallons) a day is doled out meagrely. It is no wonder soldiers collapse from thirst and exhaustion. And you haven't even done any fighting yet!

When the day's march is over, it is time to set up camp. That means selecting a site and digging a trench around it, and then using the dirt you've dug to build a wall on the outside of the trench. This is the camp's barricade against wild animals and enemy attacks. Inside you set up wooden frames with leather roofs for sleeping. Pharaoh's tent is bigger than all the others and is erected in the centre of the camp, away from danger. The officers have chairs to sit on and servants to cook for them, but you must fend for yourself.

You head into battle wearing a short kilt (a sort of skirt for men) and a leather stomach protector. Your wooden shield is covered with leather too. Depending on the regiment you are in, you may be armed with an axe, a throwing stick, a spear, a club, a sword, or a bow and arrows.

You march to war in long rows, one behind the other, your shields overlapping to form one big shield. You are face to face with the enemy, and you fight to the death. If the enemy falls, you push forward. If you fall, the foot soldier behind steps up to take your place.

Standard Bearer

As a standard bearer, you are an army officer in charge of 200 soldiers. When the army is on the march, you walk at the head of your regiment, carrying the company banner or standard. You also lead the regiment into battle with the standard. Sometimes the standard is a small statue of a god held high on a pole. Seeing it waving above their heads boosts the soldiers' morale and makes them believe the god's presence will help them fight to victory.

If you are a standard bearer, you have proven your bravery in battle and are a respected officer.

PLAN OF ATTACK

The Egyptian army was organized into companies of 200 men according to the weapons each used. The division commanders led the attack, using a tried-and-true strategy. First up were the archers and slingers, because they could shoot arrows and hurl rocks from a distance. While they were doing this, the chariots charged up and down the enemy line looking for a hole or weak spot. When they found one, the Egyptian foot soldiers charged through it, swinging their axes and clubs. The chariots were right on their heels, and together they pushed through to the rear of the enemy line. Now they had the enemy penned in. It couldn't go forward or backwards. As the Egyptian foot soldiers took care of the other army in hand-to-hand combat, the charioteers chased down any enemy troops that tried to run away.

HOME SWEET HOME

Ancient Egyptian soldiers didn't like to fight in foreign countries, because they were afraid of dying there. If their bodies weren't taken back to Egypt for burial, they would have no chance of being reborn in the next life.

Fortress Commander

All through ancient Egypt, the landscape was dotted with mud-brick fortresses surrounded by high, thick walls. Many of the strongholds were located along the Nile, close enough to help each other if any of them was attacked. These forts were quite large, and were constructed to protect the town and civilians inside. There were fortresses situated on the desert fronts too, but these were much smaller, serving as prisons, surveillance stations, and safe rest stops for travelers. They were built on hills to give them the best view of anyone coming or going. The forts were built a day's march from one another, so that when the Egyptian army was on the move, it was assured of a safe water supply. Guarding the wells and water holes in the area was an important job of the soldiers working in the fortress. Even so, enemies were sometimes successful in poisoning the wells with the dead carcasses of sheep and other animals.

If you are the fortress commander at a remote fortress outpost, you are probably counting the days—make that years—until your posting is over. You won't even mind the week-long march back to the heart of Egypt. The usual length of a posting is six years! That's a long time, but if you do your job well, Pharaoh might promote you. So you are diligent about your work. Most days all you see is sand and the soldiers under your command, but you are always on the lookout for invaders, and you question all travelers to make sure they have valid business in Egypt. On the bright side, passing merchants can often be persuaded to share their trade goods with you.

BUHEN FORT

Buhen Fort was a huge fortress built along the Nile near Egypt's southern border. It was as big as a castle and took about 15 million mud bricks to build. Its outer wall was 5 m (5.5 yards) thick! Three grown men could stand on each other's shoulders in the moat surrounding the fortress and the water would still be over their heads. Buhen Fort was home to 3,000 towns-people and 2,000 soldiers. It was used as a repair depot for boats and a checkpoint for those entering or leaving Egypt. When the Aswan Dam was built in 1964, the waters of Lake Nasser—the newly formed reservoir—completely submerged the remains of the fort.

Weapon Smith/Armorer

Egypt had a large army, and that meant a lot of weapons. That's where you come in. You are a weapon smith. You work in a factory with other weapon smiths. You craft spears, knives, swords, maces, battle axes, bows and arrows, and many other necessities of war—like battering rams for attacking fortresses. When Pharaoh goes into battle, he likes to win, and part of being victorious is having better weapons than the other army.

That means you are always improving the weapons you make. In the early days of war, axes, clubs, spears, knives, and arrowheads were made of stone. Then copper came along, and suddenly your weapons were more effective. But when Pharaoh's army met up with the Hyksos army, Egypt's copper blades were no match for the harder bronze the Hyksos were using, and so you started making bronze weapons too.

Often you take an enemy's weapons and improve them. That's what happened with the chariot—which was also a Hyksos weapon. So was the horse. And the composite bow. No wonder the Hyksos won that war. Never mind. That's all water under the bridge, because you adopted the Hyksos's weapons and made them better. Then Pharaoh's soldiers used those improved weapons to chase the Hyksos right back to Asia.

Another weapon you adopted from the enemy—the Sumerians this time—is the *khopesh*. This is a sickle-shaped sword, which is dandy for lopping off heads.

One of the weapons that has undergone the most change is the mace—a stone club with a wooden handle. The original mace had a rock fastened on the end, which had the annoying habit of falling off or shattering. (Some enemies had pretty hard heads.) But when you started using molded copper in place of the rock, the problem was solved. You drilled a hole in the copper and tapered the handle to fit inside. Then you started playing with the shape of the copper, flattening it a little to give it a blade, and the next thing you knew, you had invented the battle-axe.

When it is time to go to war, Pharaoh holds a big ceremony with all the weapons piled up in front of him. Then he gives them out to his soldiers.

Chariot Maker

When the Hyksos defeated Pharaoh's army in 1665 BC, the ancient Egyptians didn't know what had hit them. They hadn't stood a chance against the enemy's superior weapons—especially the horse-drawn chariot. Egyptian soldiers had never seen anything like it, and they had no idea how to defend against it. But it didn't take them long to adopt the chariot for their own—and make it even better.

The Egyptians got their first chariots through trade and by force. When King Thutmose III defeated the Syrians at the Battle of Megiddo in 1456 BC, he took over 900 chariots from them. No doubt Pharaoh's stable of horses got started the same way. But in no time, Egyptians were building their own chariots, breeding their own horses, and training the fiercest charioteers in the ancient world.

If you are a chariot maker, you take great pains to build a vehicle that will lead the army to victory. The Egyptian chariot was superior in many ways. Built of ash, elm, and birch, the chariots were very light. This made them speedy and easy to maneuver. The wooden axle was repositioned for greater stability and parts of it were covered with metal to cut down on friction where it rubbed on the wooden wheels. By putting six spokes in the wheels instead of four, the wheels were stronger and gave the chariot better support. Other chariots had wicker platforms, but the Egyptian chariot had a platform of leather, which made for a smoother ride. The cockpit was open at the back, in case the charioteers needed to make a fast getaway.

It takes you a long time to make a chariot, so it's no surprise they are expensive. Pharaoh provides charioteers with a team of horses, but it is up to the driver to pay for the chariot. That could be part of the reason why most charioteers are wealthy nobles.

Monumental Jobs

Ancient Egyptians were builders. They built the pyramids, of course, but they built lots of other things too. In the cities they constructed magnificent temples. In the Valley of the Kings they carved elaborate tombs out of the natural rock formations. Throughout the whole kingdom they erected monuments and statues honoring the gods and pharaohs. They even built roads and paved them with a dark, volcanic rock called basalt.

Using simple copper and bronze tools, it took years to finish these mammoth projects. It took 20 years to build the Great Pyramid. Workers had nothing more than ropes, simple levers, pulleys, ramps, wooden rollers, sledges, and flat-bottomed barges to help them move and lift the giant blocks of stone. Yet they did it, and their work has survived for thousands of years. Modern builders marvel at how the Egyptians were able to accomplish so much with so little.

THE GREAT SPHINX

Ancient Egyptian carvers turned a mountain of sandstone into a sphinx—a creature that has the body of a lion and the head of a man. The sculpture, which is six storeys high, sits like a guard in front of the great pyramids of Giza. Though the sphinx has survived a long time—except for its nose and beard—smog, humidity, and desert winds are now causing it to crumble. Unless scientists can figure out a way to stop this erosion, the Great Sphinx may one day be gone.

Engineer

Engineers are people who design machines or other structures that do work. In a way, engineers are inventors. They are always thinking *What if . . .* "*What if I built a really long wall around a marsh?*" one ancient Egyptian engineer asked. So he did and the marsh turned into much-needed farmland. The rerouted water became a reservoir.

As an engineer, it is your job to make everyone else's job easier. You develop irrigation systems to help farmers get water to their crops. You connect the Nile and the Red Sea with canals to make travel easier for merchants. For sculptors, you figure out how to move and erect obelisks (stone pillar monuments). For builders, you devise ways to get the giant building stones from the quarries to the pyramids.

IMHOTEP

Imhotep was a famous architect—*and* an engineer and doctor—who designed the Step Pyramid for Pharaoh Djoser. Though he wasn't born a nobleman, Imhotep went on to become Vizier of Egypt (that's like the prime minister) and was eventually made a god.

Climb higher!

I'm right behind you.

Hold steady.

OBELISKS

Obelisks were tall, four-sided pillars with pyramid-shaped tops. Cut from a single stone, they could weigh up to 1,000 tons (907 metric tons). They were sculpted at Pharaoh's request and were covered in hieroglyphs honoring him and the sun god, Ra. Obelisks often stood in pairs at the entrance to a temple. Obeliscus Augusti, at Heliopolis (heel-e-op-o-lis) was made of red granite and stood four giraffes high. It was a monumental task just carving it, never mind getting it to stand up! Today, there are only 26 obelisks left, and 18 of those have been taken to other countries to be put on display. There are only eight still in Egypt.

Architect

Mathematician

As an architect you are in charge of planning pyramids, palaces, temples, tombs, and even entire towns.

With the help of astronomers, you choose the location for whatever is going to be built. Then you design the building and figure out what construction materials are needed and where to get them. There is also the matter of workers. A big project might call for 15,000 men just to cut and haul stone! Painters, sculptors, and other craftspeople have to be hired too.

If you are organized and a good planner, and if you know your rock, you might want to be an architect. The best part of your job is creating the maze of tunnels, booby traps, and secret chambers inside the tombs to discourage grave robbers.

Do you like working with numbers? If so, you might want to be a mathematician. Mathematicians were scribes who specialized in math. They studied for this job in the House of Life, solving advanced math problems found in the Rhind Papyrus. This document contained everything Egyptians knew about mathematics. Ancient Egyptian mathematicians could add, subtract, multiply, and divide. They used a base 10 number system that was a lot like ours. They knew how to use fractions and find the area of rectangles, circles, and triangles.

If you are a mathematician, you are in charge of measuring the water levels of the Nile. You also calculate the size of farms and use those calculations to figure out the amount of tax farmers should pay. You know geometry, so you help architects solve building problems. You have created a standard weight system for trade, and you invented tape measures made of knotted rope. You have even attempted to calculate the exact length of a year. Who cares that you ended up with a couple of extra days?

Laborer

Stone Hauler

Architects and engineers might have been the brains behind ancient Egypt's monuments, but it was the hundreds of thousands of laborers who built them. Some of the workers were slaves, but many were actually farmers fulfilling their annual corvée.

Being a laborer is back-breaking work for you. You might haul huge stones to the structure being built, or you might throw water on the sand in front of the sledge to make the heavy load slide easier. Maybe you're one of the people who picks up the discarded hunks of rock and takes them away. Or your job might be to build ramps or dirt embankments. Whatever type of labor you do, you work in ten-day cycles—eight on and two off.

The good thing about your job is that all your needs are taken care of. Food, clothing, lodging—even your tools—are provided for you. And you are paid in grain. The bad thing about the job is that there are a lot of accidents. If you get trapped under a sledge and lose your foot, you won't be able to work anymore, and there is no accident insurance in ancient Egypt.

To be a stone hauler, you must be strong. Even so, it takes 10 men to get a single stone from the quarry to the pyramid site. Over 2 million stones were used to build the Great Pyramid of King Khufu in Giza. Some of them weighed 2 tons (1814 metric tons); some weighed as much as 70 tons (63,490 metric tons). (You might need extra help to transport those big ones.) Some quarries aren't too far from the pyramid so you might be able to get the stone—if it's a small one—where it needs to be in a couple of hours.

The stone sits on a flat sheet of wood called a sledge that you pull with ropes. The path you use is packed down to make it hard and smooth. As you haul the sledge, laborers run ahead, pouring water on the path. This makes the sledge slide more easily. Some of the finer finishing stones come from quarries farther away. These stones must be hauled by sledge to a barge that floats them down the Nile. You must then transfer them to another sledge and haul them to the pyramid. This might take a bit longer than a couple of hours!

Foreman

Water Carrier

It took thousands of people to build a tomb or a temple, and they all had different jobs. *Your* job is to make sure they do *their* jobs properly. There are many foremen at a building site. Each of you is in charge of a crew of workers. At the beginning of the day, you give your workers the tools and equipment they need, and at the end of the day, you make sure the equipment comes back in again. If you are supervising stone haulers, you might beat out a rhythm on a drum to keep them working at a good pace. If you are supervising the stone setters, you make sure the stones are fitted snugly in the proper positions. On pay day you see that each worker in your crew receives the right amount of grain.

Your job may not be glamorous, but it is very necessary. You live in Deir el-Medina, and it is your responsibility to supply the village with water. Since the village is in the desert, this means you must walk down to the Nile flood plain and back again—all day long. There are 70 households in the village with about 6 people in each house. Each person uses 18 l (4 gallons) of water a day. That's 7,560 l (1,997 gallons) of water to carry every day! It's a good thing there are five other water carriers to help you. While the other villagers head off to work at the tomb each morning, you lift your wooden yoke onto your shoulders and head to the river. On each end of the yoke is a leather bag hanging from a rope. The trip to the flood plain—when the water bags are empty—is easy, but the walk back is another story. You are hot and tired and very, very thirsty. It's a good thing you have water.

Water break, men!

DEIR EL-MEDINA
Near modern day Luxor in the Valley of the Kings, archaeologists have found the remains of a village called Deir el-Medina. This small walled village consists of one street with 70 houses. The men who worked on the tombs lived here with their families. Each house had four rooms with stone floors and whitewashed walls. There were no windows to let the sun in, just small openings in the roof. People cooked their meals outside. Deir el-Medina existed for 400 years, and during that time a total of 30,000 workers and their families lived there.

Stonemason

Stone Setter

The quarrymen break the stone away from the slab of rock. The stonemason chips it to the proper shape and size. The stone hauler moves it to the spot where it will be used. Now it is up to you to position it into place.

At the pyramid construction site, you wait for the stone to be dragged up a ramp. Then it is time to set it. It takes about 10 stone setters to maneuver one stone into place. You set the corner stones first. Then you add the stones in between—working your way to the middle. It is very important to get the stones in exactly the right position. Considering the Great Pyramid took 20 years to build, you would hate to have to start over.

You are an expert at cutting stone and know just where to chip, hammer, and wedge your chisel to split limestone, sandstone, granite, alabaster, and basalt. Using only your copper saws and wooden mallets, you whittle the enormous rocks to the shape and size needed. Some stones will be turned into statues. Others will be used to build temples. Still others will end up in pyramids and tombs. Once the stone is the way you want it, it is put on a sledge or barge and moved to the building site.

Brick Maker

Though temples, pyramids, and tombs were made of stone, all other buildings in ancient Egypt were made of mud brick—even Pharaoh's palaces. Since brick doesn't weather as well as stone, there isn't much left of these buildings. They didn't even last long in Egyptian times. People usually had to rebuild their homes every few years.

So being a brick maker is steady work. You make your bricks right on the building site, using mud, straw, sand, and water. The mud and water you get from the Nile. Between brick makers and potters, so much mud is used that Egyptians made a quarry just for mud at Wadi Hammamat. You buy straw from farmers, and, of course, the sand is everywhere. You stir these brick ingredients together and then pour the mixture into wooden molds to harden in the sun.

EGYPTIAN HOUSES

Ancient Egyptians lived in mud-brick houses. They could be one or more storeys high, but they all had flat roofs with stairs leading up, so people could use the roofs as extra places to work or sleep. The walls were whitewashed inside and out and had openings near the top to let in light. But these openings were very small so that the houses would stay cool. Wealthy people painted brightly colored pictures all over their walls. Most houses had a living area and sleeping area, but no kitchen. All the cooking was done outside. Don't even ask about bathrooms. Unless you were very rich, those were outside too.

AT YOUR DISPOSAL

There were no sewer systems and no garbage pickup in ancient Egypt. Waste disposal was the responsibility of individual citizens. Except for wealthy Egyptians, people bathed in the Nile and did their private business in a bucket outdoors. The contents of the buckets as well as all other sorts of waste were then dumped in the local irrigation canals, which became breeding grounds for rats and disease.

Scribe of Outlines

After the walls of the temples and tombs were plastered and whitewashed, the artists came in to decorate them. First was the scribe of outlines. If you have this job, you are a sort of draftsman.

You start by dipping a string in ink and stretching it over the walls to make a grid of squares. In ancient Egyptian paintings, the figures are lined up in rows, and this grid helps you to draw them straight and keep them in proportion. Once the grid is done, you use charcoal to outline the painting. It may be a scene or just a series of figures. Your job is now finished until the colorist has filled in the outlines. Then you come back to outline the figures again in red or black.

To complete the painting, a scribe writes an inscription in hieroglyphs.

Colorist

You are an artist who adds paint to the pictures. You often work by the light of an oil lamp, because you often must paint in dark places. Your paints are made from minerals such as copper, carbon, malachite, chalk, and ochre. These are ground into powder and mixed with water and beeswax to create beautiful reds, yellows, greens, blues, blacks, and whites. Your paintbrushes are sticks of wood with mushed ends. You paint solid blocks of color without any shading, and you try your best to stay inside the lines.

ANCIENT EGYPTIAN ARTISTS

Ancient Egyptian artists weren't what we think of as artists. They were more like craftspeople. They painted pictures, but their work wasn't intended to express their own personalities. It was meant to tell a story, praise the gods, or recount a person's life. Artists worked on the walls of palaces, tombs, and temples, but they couldn't paint just anything they wanted. They painted what they were told to paint, and their work was closely supervised.

There were a lot of painting rules to follow too. For instance, people were always drawn with their upper body and shoulders facing front, but with their legs facing sideways. (Not an easy way to stand.) Their heads had to face sideways too, but the eye you could see faced front.

EGYPTIAN MONUMENTS

Everyone knows the Egyptians built the pyramids, but they built many other amazing monuments as well. Here are just a few that are still standing:

- The Great Sphinx (sfinks) of Giza (geeza)
- The Temple of Karnak
- The Temple of Ramses II at Abu Simbel
- The Tombs in the Valley of the Kings
- The Luxor Temple
- The Obelisks of Thutmose I, Hatshepsut, and Thutmose III
- The Mortuary Temple of Hatshepsut

CHAPTER 3

Nile Jobs

For ancient Egyptians, the Nile was the source of all life. Each year between June and September, the river spilled its banks and sent the people fleeing for the safety of higher ground. We're talking a huge flood! It submerged over a quarter of Egypt with water as deep as a man's chest. A farmer who built his home too close to the river might watch helplessly as it washed away, knowing he had no choice but to rebuild once the river subsided—probably on the same site.

But it was worth it. As the Nile raced from the Ethiopian Mountains it picked up rich, black silt. But when the river reached the flatter lands of Egypt, it slowed down. Unable to hold the heavy soil any longer, it dropped it all over the Nile River Valley, creating the fertile soil of the black land. A particularly heavy flood would mean more people had to rebuild their houses, but it also meant bumper crops for farmers. Light floods could mean a poorer harvest and famine for everyone.

But the Nile was more than just a source of rich soil. Egyptians used its water to wash their clothes and themselves. They went out in their boats to fish and trade, and sometimes just to enjoy the sights. They watered their animals and hunted the birds, crocodiles, and hippopotamuses lurking in the papyrus marshes. And they ferried their dead pharaohs across the Nile on barges to the Valley of the Kings.

ASWAN DAM

In the 1900s, the Aswan Dam was built, stopping the flooding of the Nile forever. These days the excess water is stored in a reservoir and released as it is needed. This means that people can live on the banks of the Nile without worrying about their homes washing away. The dam also provides much-needed hydroelectricity. On the downside, the fertile, black soil ancient Egyptian farmers relied on for their crops has disappeared. Instead of rushing into the Nile Valley with the river, the soil is blocked by the dam and sits like sludge at the bottom of the reservoir. Controlling the flood waters means Egypt has 30 percent more farmland than before and crops can be grown year round, but the soil isn't as good, so neither is the quality of the crops.

Boat Builder

Ancient Egyptians used a lot of boats. That's a good thing if you're a boat builder, because you always have work.

Everybody wants one of your papyrus rafts. Made of bundles of dried reeds tied together with rope, this boat is wide in the middle with pointed ends that rise out of the water. Air pockets in the reeds keep the boat from sinking. Because it's small and easy to paddle or pole, this boat is perfect for hunting and fishing in the shallow marshes of the Nile.

You construct larger river boats too. But you have to find wood to build them first, and that isn't easy. There aren't many trees in Egypt, so you have to make do with sycamore and the brittle wood of the acacia tree. It's only when trading ships return from Lebanon with cedar or from Syria with pine that you have good wood to work with. (Lebanon and Syria are Middle East countries ancient Egypt traded with.) The river boats must be light so that they'll go fast, and shallow so that they don't get hung up on the shifting sandbanks. Most river boats have sails and oars, and some even have deck cabins made of woven mats.

Sea ships are a lot like river boats, but much wider and longer with room for 30 rowers. Funeral boats are long too and very fancy. The boats you make to carry the coffins of pharaohs and other important people are even trimmed with gold and jewels. Cattle boats and barges, on the other hand, aren't fast *or* pretty, but they're sturdy enough to carry tons of quarried stone for the pyramids.

You take pride in the work you do. You use your adze to smooth the planks and your axe and saw to cut them to length. You have a good supply of mallets, drills, and chisels too. Iron hasn't been discovered yet, so your tools are made of stone, copper, and bronze. You use copper staples and wooden rods called dowels to fasten the planks, and you smear beeswax in the joints to seal the wood against leaks. Luckily you don't have to build boats by yourself. You have other people working for you, including your son, who will take over the business after you die.

Washerman

Because Egypt is such a hot country—the average temperature in the summer months is over 38° C (100° F)—ancient Egyptians didn't wear a lot of clothes. In fact, when servants, farmers, and other laborers were working, they sometimes didn't bother with clothes at all. Children liked to go naked too. But when people did dress, they made sure their clothes were clean.

Washing clothes was a man's job. (That's right. Men did the laundry.) That might have been because scrubbing clothes required a lot of muscle. Or it might just have been because of the crocodiles. Near the river, crocodiles were always a danger, and that's where most people washed their clothes.

You are a professional washerman. Wealthy people pay you to launder their clothes. Yours is a clean job but hard work just the same. First you soak the clothes, and then—using natron, a mineral containing sodium carbonate or washing soda—you scrub them and beat them with a stick. (That will teach them to get dirty!) Most people's clothes are white linen, so stains really show up. Once the clothes are cleaned and rinsed, you twist them around a stick to squeeze out the water. The Egyptian air is so warm that it doesn't take the clothes long to dry.

During the flood season, you complete your corvée at the village of Deir el-Medina, washing the clothes of all the workers in the Valley of the Kings. The river is farther away, but at least you have the use of a donkey to carry the clothes back and forth. And, who knows—perhaps your work will come to the notice of an important official. If you do your job well, you might earn a position at the royal palace as Washer to the Pharaoh.

NILOMETER

The nilometer was invented to measure the Nile's annual flood. Nilometers were stone staircases built at different places along the river. They had marks on them to show the water level. Knowing how high the water had risen helped Egyptians predict the size of the harvest.

Reed Cutter

Fowler

Being a reed cutter is very hard work. You leave your house early in the morning and don't return until night. As you wade through the marshes, gathering papyrus reeds that are taller than you are, your back feels as if it's going to break. Your clothes get caught up in the reeds, so you work naked, and your skin bakes in the burning sun. Your eyes sting, your hands smell, and you are constantly swatting away mosquitoes and sand fleas. When you have gathered as much papyrus as you can carry, you bundle it up, hoist it onto your back, and trudge home.

There are many buyers for the reeds you gather. The shoemaker weaves them into sandals. The paper maker mashes them up for paper. The boat builder bundles them together to make boats. Wealthy Egyptians decorate their homes with the papyrus flowers, and everyone eats the tender shoots.

The marshes along the Nile are filled with geese, pigeons, plovers, ducks, owls, cranes, herons, doves, ibis, and pelicans. (Whew! That's a lot of birds.) Wealthy Egyptians like to hunt birds for sport, but you hunt them for a living; you are a fowler. Some fowlers hunt with a throw stick—a hard, curved piece of wood that looks a bit like a boomerang and turns end over end when it's thrown. Another way to hunt birds is to spread a large piece of net on the ground and bait it with fish. When the birds fly down to eat, they get tangled in the net. Or sometimes you just sneak up on the birds and throw a net over them.

Though you usually sell the birds you catch, you sometimes take ducks, pigeons, and geese home to fatten them up.

Fisherman

The Nile is full of fish, and it is your job to catch them. Some days you go out on the river in your papyrus boat, bait your copper hook, and drop your line into the water. As you wait, you watch the water—not for perch or carp, but for hippopotamuses. They like to walk along the bottom of the river and come up under unsuspecting boats. If you get dumped, you not only get wet and lose your catch, you become lunch for the hippo!

Some days you fish with a friend. Dragging a mesh basket made of papyrus reed twine between your boats, you wait for an eel or catfish to swim into it. Once in, the fish are trapped, and all you have to do is dump them into one of your boats. The easiest fishing is during *Shemu*, when the Nile waters recede. As the river shrinks, the fish are left flopping on the banks and all you have to do is pick them up. But do keep an eye out for crocodiles!

You sell your catch at the outdoor market. Your customers are mainly poor people, who can't afford to pay much. But that's all right. You can't pay much for the things you need either. A baker gives you a loaf of bread and you give him a fish. It's a fair trade. You salt and dry the fish you don't sell. Then you pack them in ashes so they won't spoil.

Ferryman

There were very few bridges in Egypt—and none long enough to span the Nile, which meant the only way to get to the other side was by boat. But not everyone owned a boat, so when they needed to cross the river they took a ferry. In the dry season, when the waters were at their lowest, people could wade across some of the shallower parts—if they were willing to risk meeting up with hippos or crocodiles, that is. But during the flood season, fording the river at any point was impossible.

This is where you come in. You are a ferryman. You may have your own boat or you might work for a wealthy nobleman who has a duty to help people without boats cross the river. Depending on the size of your ferry, you operate the sail and oars yourself or you have two or more oarsmen working for you. Passengers often bring chickens, goats, and other animals on board with them, so be prepared for some crowded—and smelly—trips. Because there are ferries sailing from different places along the Nile all day long, it is easy to catch a ride no matter where a person lives—as long as it's daylight. You never sail after dark. For one thing, you can't see the treacherous, shifting sandbanks, and you don't want to hit one. For another thing, night is when the dead are said to wander about, and you don't want to run into them either!

Black Land Jobs

E gypt belonged to Pharaoh. He owned it. All of it. Every papyrus reed, every head of cattle, every nugget of gold, every grain of wheat—it was all Pharaoh's. He did share though. Especially the land. Not the desert so much. Nobody was too interested in red land real estate—except for the gold mines, and Pharaoh wasn't willing to share those. It was the black land that people wanted. However, it was mostly just the nobles and temple priests who got any.

Black land workers—people like farmers and herders—used the land but they didn't own it. Sometimes they rented it, and sometimes they worked on the estates of wealthy nobles. The jobs they did fed everyone in Egypt, and without them, people would have starved. The strange thing is that the black land workers were the ones most likely to go hungry. After they paid their taxes and made offerings to the gods, they had very little left.

Bee Keeper

Since ancient Egyptians didn't have sugar, honey was used to sweeten food. It was also used for making beer, wine, medicine, and perfume. It was given as an offering to the gods and it was even put in dead people's graves—in case they got hungry in the afterlife. Honey never goes bad, so when King Tut's tomb was opened in 1923, the honey inside was still good! Nobody ate it though.

Beeswax had uses too. It thickened paint and kept boats from leaking. Sculptors used it when making molds for metal statues, and it was used on wigs to keep the curls in place. Rich Egyptians even put it on their heads! At parties guests were given cones to wear on their wigs. The cones were made of beeswax, animal fat, and flower essence. During the party the cones would melt from the heat, and the guests would smell like flowers. They must have been pretty sticky though.

If you are a beekeeper, you probably live and work in Lower Egypt (that's the northern bit), because the bee is the symbol for that part of the country. And—of course—you live where there are lots of flowers. You keep your bees in woven-reed hives with a hole in the front for the bees to come and go. These hives are covered in baked clay and stacked on their sides. When it's time to collect the honey, you take the back off the hive and remove the honeycombs. To keep the bees from stinging you, your helper uses smoke to send the bees to the front of the hive.

Even though you have your own bees, you sometimes collect honey from wild bees. That's a bit more work and also more dangerous. If you'd been a beekeeper in the early days of ancient Egypt you would always have been on the move. Those beekeepers put the hives in their papyrus boats and followed the flowers. Wherever the flowers were blooming, that's where the beekeepers were—and the bees.

Farmer

A farmer's day is long. In the morning you get up, put on your kilt, then wash and shave. Your wife puts on a loose linen dress and slips a lucky amulet around her neck. Then she lights the fire and grinds the wheat for bread. Breakfast is simple—bread and beer—and then to work.

It is planting season. Yesterday Pharaoh's scribes measured your land (so that they'll know how much to tax you at harvest time) and gave you seeds. Your main crops are wheat, barley, and flax, but you also plant vegetables. Sometimes you can harvest as many as three vegetable crops in a single year because of the long growing season .

To plant the grain, you first scatter the seed. Then you hitch your cow to a wooden plough and cut shallow furrows or ruts in the soil. When that's done you get your pigs to trample the seed into the ground.

As your crops grow, you weed and water them. Weeding in the hot sun is tiring work. Watering is even harder. There are no sprinklers in ancient Egypt. Not even a hose. So you must use the *shaduf* to bring water to your fields from the ditches and canals. When you are not weeding and watering, you are chasing away birds and insects.

Everyone helps with the harvest. Using wooden sickles with flint teeth, you and the other farmers cut the grain. Then the cattle trample it out of the husks. The women finish the job by throwing the grain into the air. This is called winnowing. The grain is stored in sacks, and the straw that is left is put aside for making mud bricks.

When the harvest season ends, and you have paid your taxes, it is time to repair your tools and shore up the ditches and canals around your fields. You hardly finish before the Nile starts flooding its banks and Pharaoh's scribes send you away to complete your annual corvée. When you return it is time to plant again.

Herder

In ancient Egypt, animals were very important. Some—like gazelles and oryx (that's a type of antelope)—were raised for their hides. Cattle, goats, and sheep were raised for their meat and milk. Donkeys were valued as pack animals, and oxen because they could do heavy work. Some animals—like the Apis Bull—were raised simply because people thought they were gods.

You are a cattle herder. You are very fond of your cows, and you give them names. You even sleep beside them. In the morning you take them out to the pasture to graze, but at night you bring them back to the safety of the cow shed. The nobleman you work for is very rich and has entire fields planted in clover just for the cattle. Sometimes you take the cattle great distances to graze, which means you are gone for weeks. All that walking combined with little to eat keeps you lean. You carry very few supplies when you travel—usually just food, a few pots, and a rolled mat on a stick to keep off the sun and wind.

You take excellent care of your herd. You milk them, look after them when they're hurt or sick, and help birth their calves. When it is time to fatten them up, you feed them boiled dough. Cattle are very valuable. If anything happens to them, you have to answer to the tax collector as well as your master. The tax collector counts the animals in your herd at the start of the year and at the end. If an animal is missing, you must produce its hide to prove that you didn't steal it.

APIS BULL

The Apis Bull was the sacred animal of the god, Ptah. To honor Ptah, a living bull was kept in the city of Memphis. But not just any bull. The black Apis Bull had a white diamond on its forehead and an eagle shape on its back. When a calf with these markings was born, Egyptians took it as a sign that a god (besides Pharaoh) had come to live among them. So when the Apis Bull died, it was a very sad time. The bull was mummified and buried in a sacred place, and all of Egypt went into mourning—until the next Apis Bull was born.

Vintner

You are a vintner. You make wine. Since only wealthy people can afford wine, you work for a nobleman who has a winery on his estate.

Sometimes you make red wine; sometimes white. Sometimes you even make wine from pomegranates and dates. But mostly you use grapes. You plant your vineyard (grape garden) on the top of a hill, because that's the best place. Grapes grow on floppy vines, so you put posts in the ground to prop them up. Every day you go to the vineyard to check the grapes and water them. They grow quickly in the Egyptian heat.

When they're ripe, you and your helpers pick them and put them in large baskets. These baskets are emptied into huge vats where a group of men stomp the grapes to a pulp. The juice from the crushed grapes is poured into large pottery jars to ferment (turn into wine). This is when you add honey or spices for flavor. When the wine is ready to drink, you strain it, pour it into smaller jars and seal them. Then you attach a label with the name of the nobleman's estate, the type of wine, when it was made, and the name of the vintner (that's you). But before the wine can be sold, the Royal Sealer of Wine has to inspect your work.

CHAPTER 5

Red Land Jobs

The desert is one of the main reasons ancient Egypt survived for 3,000 years. It was hot and dry with nothing but sand and rock everywhere you looked. Nobody wanted to live there. Heck—nobody even wanted to visit! And that was a good thing.

You see, in those days, countries were always having wars and conquering one another. But because of the desert, Egypt was harder to attack. Armies from other countries often took one look at all that sand and headed off to conquer some other place.

Egyptians found the desert a challenge too, so for a while they didn't go conquering much either, but over time they did find ways to make the desert work for them. They dug wells and protected them with fortresses so that when Egyptians *had* to be in the desert they could get water. They learned how to dig out the limestone and granite at the desert's edge and build with it. They also discovered minerals, metals, and gems buried beneath the sand and mined them to make tools, weapons, and other things they needed.

One of the best things the Egyptians discovered about the desert is that its hot, dry climate was perfect for preserving things. That's why the many tombs and all the things inside them have survived for thousands of years.

Miner

Quarryman

Mining is so difficult and dangerous that not many Egyptians want to do it. Most miners are slaves or criminals. (Mining is the penalty for their crimes. Sometimes a criminal's whole family is forced to work at a mine.)

The mines are usually in the desert and hard to get to. You must walk there with donkeys carrying heavy loads of tools and food. But your caravan is well guarded. Pharaoh does not want desert thieves to steal the gems and metals you dig up. At the mining site you live in a village of huts surrounded by a wall. There is a well, but the water in it is so foul it is almost worse than going thirsty. With nothing but an oil lamp and the reflection from bronze mirrors to help you see, you climb deep underground to hammer the rock and pick at it to find metal or gems. It is hot, dirty work. Children climb down too, collect the ore, and haul it back to the surface in baskets where men and women who are too old or lame to work underground pound it into pieces and wash off the dirt.

At the end of the day, each forced laborer receives 10 small loaves of bread and a third of a jug of beer for their work.

It is your job to cut the huge stone blocks that will be used for monuments, statues, temples, and tombs. Most limestone quarries are located where the red land and black land meet. These quarries are in the open air. You have to scrape away a layer of ground to get to them, but at least you don't have to tunnel inside a mountain as you do when quarrying granite. There are thousands of workers at the quarry—stonemasons, laborers, and quarrymen like you, but also overseers, scribes, and other government officials. You all live in a walled village of mud-brick huts.

Quarrying is a back-breaking job even though there are sometimes as many as 100 quarrymen working on a single stone. With your bronze chisels and wooden mallets, you chip a wide groove around the block of stone you want to cut. Then you hammer wooden wedges into the grooves and pull on them until the stone breaks free. (Watch your toes!)

After that the laborers haul the stone away, and you start work on the next one.

Hunter

Hunting Guide

Hunting is dangerous but exciting work. One of the animals you hunt is the hippo that lives in the marshes beside the Nile. Hippos might look slow and lazy, but you aren't fooled. You've seen a grouchy hippo chomp a full-grown crocodile in half with one bite! In your papyrus boats, you and several other hunters separate a hippo from the herd. You do this in the shallows, so the hippo can't go underwater. When you have it on its own, you tangle it in barbed ropes. The more it struggles, the deeper the barbs go.

Mostly you hunt on foot in the desert with other hunters and your dog. You go for long periods and camp in the wilderness. You use spears, nets, and arrows. To snare wild hares you use wood traps. On the grass-lands south of Egypt you hunt ostriches. Ostrich eggs are a delicacy and wealthy Egyptians will pay a lot for them. Sometimes you go even farther south to hunt elephant, wild bull, and lion. These animals are especially dangerous, and though you are good at your job, you still ask the gods to make you successful and keep you from harm.

As a hunting guide, you do all the same things a hunter does—but you work with amateurs. Instead of hunting with other hunters, you take groups of wealthy nobles hunting. Sometimes they even bring their wives and children along. The noble hunters' favorite weapon is a throw stick, but you make sure there are also lots of bows and arrows, traps, nets, lassos, and spears on hand—just in case. You take along a few hyenas too. Hyenas have a really strong odor that keeps the animals you are hunting from picking up your scent. Of course, you have your pack of hunting dogs as well. They sniff out the wild pig or whatever animal you are tracking and drive it into the open. Nobles like to hunt lions best. Pharaoh uses a chariot when he hunts, but even he isn't safe from a charging lion. So he keeps several attendants on hand to stand between him and the lion.

Merchant/Trader

The Nile Valley was a good place to live, but it didn't provide ancient Egyptians with everything. So it was up to merchants to go to other lands and bring back the things Egyptians needed.

Merchants had a code of ethics—things they should and should not do. Every merchant knew the value of the goods they were trading, and it was unethical to undercut the competition by selling something for less than it was worth. It was also bad ethics to stockpile merchandise, and even worse to lie about how much business you'd done in order to pay less tax.

The most trustworthy traders worked for Pharaoh, traveling to nearby Asian and African countries to get the things he wanted. Often they took gifts from Pharaoh to give to the kings of the countries they were visiting. This was a gesture of friendship, but the expensive presents also showed how rich and powerful Pharaoh was. Naturally the kings sent bigger and better presents back. (Pharaoh wasn't so dumb.)

Sometimes merchants packed their goods in big sea ships and headed out into the Mediterranean and the Red Sea. Other times they loaded trade goods and supplies onto donkeys and trekked across the desert in caravans. Either way, they were well guarded.

If you like to barter and travel (and you don't get seasick or sunstroke), a merchant might be the job for you.

Robber

You might not think being a robber is a job, but stealing is how some ancient Egyptians made a living. Most people didn't set out to be robbers. They worked at other things. But then for some reason they stole an offering to the gods or a sack of grain, and the next thing they knew they were stealing full time.

If you are a robber, you might live in the desert hills in a hidden cave and steal from travelers. Or you might hold down a job building tombs during the day and be a grave robber at night. The tombs of wealthy Egyptians are filled with treasure, and even though tomb robbers would be cursed by the gods, you rob the graves anyway.

Tombs aren't easy to get into. You can try to chip your way in with a chisel, but a faster way is to light a fire against the tomb wall, and when it's good and hot, throw cold water on it. The sudden change in temperature makes the rock wall crack.

Once inside, you use candles to light your way through the tomb's tunnels. When you find the mummy, you unwrap it and remove rings and other jewelry. You might even set fire to the wooden coffin to melt the gold on it. You take as many treasures as you can carry away.

Whatever you do, don't get caught at work. The penalties for stealing are not fun. If you steal only a small thing, the judge might simply make you give it back and pay a fine. A bigger crime might earn you a beating with a cane, or you could be branded with a hot iron. The worse the crime, the more horrible the punishment. You could be sent to work in the mines, or you could have your hand or nose lopped off. You could even be sentenced to death and get thrown on a sharp stake. (Ouch!) The worst part is that your body might not be buried, and that means no afterlife for you.

CHAPTER 6

Noble Jobs

Nobles were the well-to-do citizens of ancient Egypt. Their status was inherited, and many of them were royalty, which meant they were related to Pharaoh. Naturally they were all very wealthy and lived in fine houses on huge estates. They had hundreds of people working for them. Compared to most Egyptians, nobles lived very comfortable lives. They had elegant clothes and fine jewelry, and enjoyed every luxury a person could imagine. Nobles never went hungry. They never quarried stone or dug canals. They hunted and fished, took picnics on the Nile, threw banquets, and attended sporting events. They listened to poetry and music, and played games.

That doesn't mean nobles didn't work. They did. If you are a noble, you get the best jobs in Egypt. You probably hold an important job in the government. You might work as a building overseer of a big monument, or perhaps you are a *nomarch*. Maybe you are a commander in the army or one of Pharaoh's personal attendants. If you are a woman, you could work part-time as a priestess or be a nursemaid in one of the royal households.

Regardless of their job, nobles still had to fulfill the responsibilities of being nobles. Egypt ran smoothly for 3,000 years, because everyone had a place and knew what was expected of them. Being a noble was certainly easier than being a reed cutter or quarryman, but it was still a job.

FAMOUS PHARAOHS

Narmer—he was the first pharaoh of ancient Egypt

Djoser—he commanded the building of Egypt's first pyramid

Khufu—he commanded the building of the Great Pyramid at Giza

Pepi II—Egypt's longest reigning pharaoh at 96 years

Hatshepsut—she was the longest-ruling female pharaoh

Thutmose III (Tut-moz)—he made Egypt a huge empire by conquering other countries

Amenhotep III (Ah-men-hoe-tep)—he was responsible for building many monuments and temples

Akhenaten (Ak-nat-n)—he started a new religious belief in one god, the sun god, Aten

Tutankhamen—he was a child king whose tomb was undisturbed for thousands of years

Ramses the Great (Ram-zeez)—he ruled for 67 years and was one of Egypt's greatest warriors

Cleopatra—she was the last pharaoh of ancient Egypt

Pharaoh

Chief Wife

When Narmer united Upper and Lower Egypt, he put the two old crowns together to make a new one called the double crown of Egypt.

No matter where Pharaoh went, he stood out in a crowd. The crown had a lot to do with that. Then there was the bull's tail hanging from his belt, as well as the shepherd's staff and fly whisk that he carried. When he went to war, he put on a bright blue helmet crown.

If you land the job of Pharaoh, the first thing you have to do is bury the pharaoh who just died. Since he was probably your father, you'll want to give him a grand funeral to show people what a great pharaoh he was—and how rich you are.

As Pharaoh, it is up to you to keep law and order, protect Egypt from invasion, and lead religious festivals. If the gods are happy they will grant a good harvest. There are religious duties to take care of, documents to read, requests to hear, and foreign visitors to entertain. Don't forget the Nile—you have to keep track of the water levels and check on the progress of the harvest. You must visit the cities throughout Egypt and the army outposts too. Then, of course, there is your family to consider. You have many wives and even more children. The word "pharaoh" means palace or great house, and with a family the size of yours, you *need* a palace!

Though Pharaoh has many wives, he singles one out as his favorite. You are known as the King's Chief Wife or Great Wife. You are expected to be by Pharaoh's side at all times and silently support him. You also take part in important religious ceremonies.

During the early days of ancient Egypt, you lived in the palace harem (women's living quarters) with Pharaoh's other wives. But over time, you have become more independent and powerful and now have a home and servants of your own.

Your most important job is to have lots of children. The more sons, the better. The Chief Wife's son usually becomes the next pharaoh, but if you have no son, the honor might go to one of Pharaoh's other wives, and you wouldn't want that. If Pharaoh dies and your son becomes Pharaoh while he is still a child, you rule in his name until he is old enough to do so himself.

Pharaoh's Mother

Royal Princess

You are one of Pharaoh's lesser wives and because of that you are an honored person in Egyptian society. You live in the harem of one of Pharaoh's palaces. The harem is very large, because it must house many wives, their children, and servants. It is a hive of activity and gossip. Some royal princesses are daughters of foreign kings. Some are Egyptian noble-women. Your greatest hope is that your son will become the next pharaoh.

Mother of a pharaoh was a highly respected position. It was as close as a person could get to the gods without actually being one. You have your own big house and servants to fulfill all your wants and needs. Egyptians believed Pharaoh's mother had the power to send forth sacred energy, so you are often found near Pharaoh on important occasions. Pharaoh privately consults with you and his Chief Wife on matters of State.

Great Royal Daughter

See you later, sis.

CHILDREN'S GAMES

Children in ancient Egypt entertained themselves much as children today do. One of their favorite games was tug-of-war. Another was *khuzza-lawizza*, an Egyptian version of leapfrog. However, instead of jumping over each other, the players leapt over their playmates' outstretched arms.

Pharaoh is your father and his Chief Wife is your mother. You are their eldest daughter. You live a pampered life in your mother's palace. Your job is to marry the next pharaoh. In other words, you will marry your brother. This will strengthen Pharaoh's claim as king, because it doubles the amount of royal blood he brings to the throne.

SENET

Ancient Egyptians liked to play board games, and Senet was one of their favorites. It was a bit like backgammon. The board was arranged in three rows of ten squares, and the players raced around the squares to the finish line. Throw sticks were used like dice.

Nobleman

Noblewoman

You are very rich. You live in a huge villa on 2 to 3 acres (about a hectare) of land. Your house has 20 rooms—even a bathroom with a toilet your servants empty, and a bathing area where they pour buckets of water over you. Outside you wander through the orchards, ponds, and beautiful gardens. There is even a small shrine where you can worship the local god. Your estate is surrounded by a high wall. Many servants and slaves work for you. They farm the land, tend your animals, brew your beer, make your wine, cook your food, and weave cloth for your clothes. Your furniture is made of the finest wood, inlaid with silver and jewels. You have your own trading ships and merchants to do your bidding.

You probably have an important government job. You may even work part-time as a priest.

Even though you live a pampered life, you still have responsibilities. You must provide transportation across the Nile for those who can't afford it, and you must host banquets to celebrate special occasions. Is this a job you think you could do?

Like all women of ancient Egypt, your most important job is to look after your home and have children. The difference between you and a farmer's wife is that your children aren't expected to help in the fields, so you don't need to have quite so many of them. This frees you up to do other things.

Your day begins with servants helping you bathe and dress. Your gauzy gown is made of the finest linen. You have a hairdresser to coif your hair, a manicurist to paint your nails, and a cosmetician to apply your makeup. Expensive jewelry is the finishing touch.

You oversee your servants as they clean your home and mind your children. Then perhaps you listen to music, play a board game, or walk through your gardens. Some days you go for a boat ride on the Nile to enjoy the scenery with friends. In the evenings you probably go to a party.

It's a tough job, but somebody has to do it.

CHAPTER 7

Assisting Pharaoh Jobs

Pharaoh was a king and a god. That meant he had a lot of power. He also had a lot of employees. Naturally he needed workers to look after his palaces and estates, but there were also officials who ran the government, priests who ran the temples, generals who ran the army, and lots and lots of overseers who ran everything else. Overseers were like managers. They didn't actually have to do any work; they just had to make sure everyone else did. Whenever a noble did something that pleased Pharaoh, he would give the noble a gold trinket or piece of land as a reward, and he would also make the noble an overseer.

Fan Bearer

Fan Bearer -to-the-Right- of-the-King

As you know, ancient Egypt was a very warm place—without air conditioning. One way to keep cool was to wave a fan.

You wouldn't expect Pharaoh to wave his own fan though—after all he is a god—so you do it for him. You work with another fan bearer. You each carry large, long-handled fans of ostrich feathers. You also carry a bouquet of flowers. When Pharaoh is making a public appearance, one of you walks ahead of him and one of you walks behind. As you move you wave the fans and flowers. This not only keeps Pharaoh cool but also gives him beautifully perfumed air to breathe.

You might think that working this close to the pharaoh would win you respect, but the truth is your place in society is lower than a servant and just above a slave. But you do stay cool and smell good.

You carry a small fan and a tiny bouquet of flowers, but they are just for show. You don't have to wave them at anybody. You don't walk in front of Pharaoh or behind him either. You are a noble, and the "to-the-right-of-the-king" part of your title indicates that you are a high-ranking official and one of Pharaoh's favorite nobles. Unless you are allergic to feathers or flowers, this is not a tough job to do.

Keeper of the Royal Seal

Sandal Bearer

Seal bearers kept track of Pharaoh's finances. They were members of his treasury department. Bearing his seal meant they had Pharaoh's authority to run his granary, his storehouses, his trading ships—in fact, all his businesses.

As Keeper of the Royal Seal all the other seal bearers answer to you. You answer to the vizier. Once a month you gather your seal bearers together and you give the vizier a report of all the income and expenses for Pharaoh's businesses.

Pharaoh's sandals were very important to him, so if you are his sandal bearer, you are pretty important too—probably Pharaoh's brother or even his son. Pharaoh didn't wear his sandals all the time, so it is your job to hold them when they aren't on his feet. This means that you go everywhere with Pharaoh, and people show you a great deal of respect. Of course, you show respect to Pharaoh too. You kiss his big toe every time you help him on with his sandals.

Magician

Ancient Egyptians knew a lot about science and mathematics, but that didn't stop them from believing in magic too. After all, it was important to stay on the right side of the gods. There was no telling what would happen if you made them angry. Even though Pharaoh was a god himself, he didn't want to take any chances either.

This is where you come in. As a magician, it is your job to help Pharaoh interpret signs and make decisions that will please the gods. You provide Pharaoh with amulets and other lucky objects. You chant spells to ensure a good crop. You look into the future and make predictions, and you cast spells against Pharaoh's enemies and any evil spirits that might be causing problems.

Our future is dark, Pharaoh.

OVERSEER JOBS

Most overseers had fancy titles but did very little work.

The Two Legs of the Lord of the Two Lands—a high-paid messenger

One Who Accompanies the Lord of the Two Lands in Every Place—Pharaoh's traveling buddy

Overseer of the Royal Toe Nail Clippings—in charge of . . . well, you know

Intendant of the Pure Place—in charge of the king's tomb

Keeper of the Secrets of the Butchering Hall—in charge of guarding Pharaoh's secret recipes

Herdsman of Dappled Cattle—in charge of the herders who herded spotted cows

Overseer of the Linen—supervised Pharaoh's weavers

His Majesty's Lieutenant-Commander of Chariotry—in charge of Pharaoh's chariots

CHAPTER 8

Government Jobs

The nobles of ancient Egypt held all the important government jobs. They were judges, governors, army officers, and advisors to Pharaoh. Government officials were well-educated—most had gone to school from age 6 to 14. They could read and write and were knowledgeable about other lands and people. Inscriptions on some of the tombs show that during a lifetime, a noble might hold as many as 20 different positions—some of them at the same time.

The government was in charge of making sure Egypt ran smoothly. It built roads and irrigation canals. It kept law and order and protected Egypt from invasion. It promoted trade and industry. It fed the people in times of drought. It supervised the construction of tombs, temples, and monuments. The government gave Egypt structure and organization.

Judge/Magistrate

GUILTY!

In ancient Egypt, minor disputes between citizens were usually decided by a village council. All other legal matters were settled by nomarchs, the vizier, or Pharaoh. A nomarch heard the cases for his nome. More serious offences might be judged by a group of nomarchs. Major crimes went to the vizier, and the really super-bad offences—like murder and tomb robberies—were taken to Pharaoh himself. There were no lawyers to argue the cases to help defend the accused person, and no juries to decide the verdict. The magistrates asked the questions—sometimes with the help of a stick! They also decided the verdict and set the punishment.

As a magistrate you wear a gold chain with a pendant of Maat, the goddess of truth and justice.

Vizier

Nomarch

Next to Pharaoh, you are the most powerful person in Egypt. You are in charge of running the government, and since white is the color of purity, you wear a long, white robe to show that you perform your duties fairly. You appoint officials and enforce the laws. You manage the country's irrigation systems and count all the people for the census. You supervise industries such as mining and trading. As Controller of the Archives you make sure that important legal matters are written down. As Master of Works you oversee the construction of royal monuments. Perhaps your most important job is collecting taxes to pay for everything. (Pyramids aren't cheap, you know!)

Pharaoh gives you generous gifts of land to show his appreciation for your hard work, and by Egyptian standards, you are rich.

Egypt was divided into 42 districts, or provinces, called nomes. These nomes were ruled by governors called nomarchs.

Being a nomarch is an important job—a bit like being a Pharaoh but on a smaller scale. Also, you are not a god. You inherited the title of nomarch from your father, but if Pharaoh doesn't like the job you're doing, he can replace you. So you make sure the nome runs smoothly and no complaints get back to the king. You have a huge estate and live a life of ease. You oversee the collection of taxes. You organize and supervise major building projects. Not all by yourself, of course. You have a large staff to help you. You are in charge of law and order and hear local court cases. You even have your own army, though you have to hand it over to Pharaoh if he needs it.

Tax Collector

Overseer of the Royal Treasury

You are a government scribe. It is your job to collect taxes from the people of Egypt. After the flooding of the Nile each year, you mark the boundaries of all the farms with stones, and you calculate how much seed to give each farmer based on the size of his land. You write everything down, so that when you return at harvest time you know how much tax to charge. Each farmer must give 20 percent of his crop as tax. A herder's tax is based on the number of animals he has.

You go house to house, collecting taxes, and you give each person a receipt to prove they've paid. The receipt is probably written on a broken piece of pottery. If a person doesn't want to pay what he owes, you beat him with a big stick to encourage him to change his mind. At the end of the day, you take all the tax you've collected (it's usually in grain) and turn it in to the Treasurer. Lucky for you, scribes don't have to pay tax.

Overseer of the Royal Treasury is a very powerful position. If you have this job, Pharaoh must really like you. You are in charge of Egypt's wealth, and since Egypt's wealth comes from the land, it is your job to give Pharaoh written reports on how the land is being used. It is also your job to make sure taxes are collected. And last, but not least, it is you who supervises the construction and furnishing of the pharaoh's tomb in the Valley of the Kings. So, how do you tell Pharaoh he can't afford the gold death mask?

Pharaoh will be pleased.

A good harvest means a wealthy treasury.

CHAPTER 9

Temple Jobs

Egyptian temples were huge buildings with tall, carved columns and high ceilings painted with stars. The interior walls were painted too, but in brightly colored illustrations and inscriptions honoring the god. Since the only windows were at the top of the walls, temples tended to be dark. Outside was a courtyard where people could leave offerings for the god. Student priests worked in the front part of the temple. The other priests worked in the inner temple. At the very back was a sacred room where a statue of the god was kept. No one but the high priest could enter this shrine.

Temples were part of large complexes that were like miniature walled towns. They had beautiful gardens, small lakes, farms, and all kinds of buildings to store the offerings people left. They even had wineries and kept animals. Temple estates were actually businesses, employing hundreds of people. But temples weren't open to the public. There were no religious services, and Egyptian citizens were not allowed to go inside. On festival days (days of religious celebration) the priests would bring the god's statue outside and walk among the crowds with it, but otherwise the temple was devoted to serving the god—not the public.

Many people worked in the temples. Naturally there were priests and priestesses. But there were also doctors and chemists. Scribe schools were located in the temples because that's where the libraries were. The study of the stars was closely linked to the gods, so astronomers worked in the temples too.

Priest

Priestess

If you are a priest, you are a servant of the gods. Your main job is to look after the temple and make offerings to the temple's god. You also oversee religious ceremonies, festivals, and funerals, supervise the work of artists, and teach in the House of Life.

Your day starts at dawn with a bath in the temple lake. You actually bathe three times a day. (Talk about clean!) Then you put on your white, linen robe. You aren't allowed to wear wool even if you're cold—it was considered unclean. Now it's time to walk through the temple with the other priests. As you move along, you burn incense, sprinkle water, and say prayers to scare off any evil spirits that might be hanging around. When you get to the room where the idol (a statue or image) of the god is kept, you wait in the hallway while the high priest (he's the one with a leopard skin over his robe) goes inside. He "wakes up" the idol, then washes and dresses it. After that he puts out food, says a few prayers, and burns incense. Then he leaves. You make this trek at lunch and supper too. At the end of the day, you all walk back to the shrine for a fourth time and wait as the high priest puts the idol to bed. Before you leave, the door is sealed with clay so that no one can enter during the night.

Most priests work part-time and take turns living in the temple—one month on, then three off. That's just three months of priest work a year. The rest of the time priests work at other jobs. Mostly they are government officials, doctors, lawyers, judges, and merchants. None of them are slaves though. That's a full-time job.

Priestesses lived in the temples devoted to goddesses, and like the priests, they worked part-time. They were usually rich noblewomen, who had servants to run their homes when it was their turn to be priestesses.

You do some of the same jobs as priests, but you do some different ones too. You take care of the temple, tend the goddess's statue, and organize the offerings. You also supervise the people who work on the temple estate. You book musicians for the religious ceremonies, and you sing, dance, shake a metal rattle called a sistrum, and act out stories during temple rituals.

If you have experience planning events and you're not shy about performing in public, priestess might be the job for you.

Astronomer

Interpreter of Dreams

If you are an astronomer, you study the stars. Your observations have led you—or other astronomers—to invent a calendar and a water clock. A water clock is a container with a hole in the bottom that allows the water to leak out; the level of the water indicates the time. One of your tools is a *merkhet*—a sighting device made from a palm leaf rib. It helps you find north, south, east, and west. Since pyramids and temples have to line up with certain stars, architects ask you where they should build. You also make maps to show all the star pictures or constellations in the night sky.

Your main job is to predict the Nile's annual flood. Considering everyone knows it's Pharaoh's godly powers that bring on the flood waters, people should ask *him* when it's going to start. But they don't. Not that it matters. You know that when the dog star, Sirius, rises in the sky before the sun does, the flood is on its way. Since most Egyptians don't know anything about reading the stars, they think you are very clever.

When ancient Egyptians have puzzling dreams, they go to the temple to see you, the interpreter of dreams. With the help of a dream book, you tell them what their dreams mean. Dreams could be reflections of things going on in the dreamers' lives, or they might show dreamers what dead people are doing. Egyptians believed that dreams were the gods' way of looking into their hearts. If dreams show something bad is going to happen, you give the dreamers a spell to recite as they eat fish and herbs dipped in beer. (Imagine the dreams they have after that!) If people are having problems, they can sleep in one of the temple buildings and get their dreams interpreted first thing in the morning.

If you have a good imagination, you might like to be an interpreter of dreams.

THE DREAM BOOK SAYS . . .
Seeing yourself in a dream could mean all sorts of things. If you are diving into cold water, it means you are being forgiven for all your bad deeds. If you dream your face is touching the ground, it means the dead want something. (Uh-oh.) But if you see yourself dead, it means you are going to have a long life. (Go figure.)

Scribe

You are a professional writer. You write reports. You write religious scrolls, songs, stories, and poetry. You also write letters and other documents for people who don't know how to read and write. In ancient Egypt, that was most everybody. And that makes you a bit of a snob. You think you are better than workers in other occupations. You don't worry about going hungry, you don't get dirty, you don't have to do hard labor, and you have the means to improve your station in life. You don't have to perform a corvée and you don't have to pay tax.

Some scribes work for the government, keeping mining records, collecting taxes, or ordering supplies for the army. Others make lists of the offerings at a temple or keep the accounts for a large estate.

Every morning you put on your white linen kilt, gather your reed brushes, papyrus scrolls, the wooden board that holds your inks, grinder, and water pot and head off to work. Your office is wherever you are. You just sit down cross-legged on a stool or the ground and use your lap as a table.

You started scribe school when you were six and spent eight years studying hieroglyphs. You had to learn over 800 symbols. Compared to the 26 letters in our alphabet, that's a lot. Each day you took your lunch of bread and beer and headed off to school, where you memorized and copied stories and other documents. Your desk was the floor. Papyrus paper is expensive, so you did your lessons on broken pottery called *ostraca*. But you worked very hard. You didn't want to earn any bruises from the teacher's stick for being lazy.

ROSETTA STONE

Egyptians left lots of written records about their civilization, but because they were in hieroglyphs, modern people couldn't read them. Until 1799, that is. That's when a stone found near the Egyptian town of Rosetta solved the hieroglyphic mystery. The Rosetta Stone contained a story in three different languages—hieroglyphs, Demotic (another kind of Egyptian writing), and Greek. Historians used the Greek story to figure out the hieroglyphic symbols.

HIEROGLYPHS

Hieroglyphs is a type of picture writing that uses about 800 different symbols. Some of those symbols stand for consonants or the sounds consonants make. For instance, an owl represents the letter M and a basket represents both C and K because both those letters make the same sound. The Egyptians had no symbols for vowels. Other hieroglyphs stand for the combined sound of letters, such as CH or SH, and others just represent objects or ideas. The word *kheper* (kef-fer) means *becoming, existing,* or *evolving* and is shown as a scarab or beetle.

Teacher

Pharmacist

If you are a teacher you are probably also a priest. You may hold classes in the House of Life or you might have them right in your own home. Mostly your students are the sons of wealthy Egyptians, though sometimes they include the sons of kings from other countries or even the sons of poorer Egyptians who have saved enough to pay. You don't usually teach girls though. They get lessons in homemaking from their mothers.

You teach geography, mathematics, history, reading, and writing. You read stories and poems and have your students write them down. Sometimes you teach foreign languages. You also teach your students to respect adults and be polite to strangers, and you keep a stick handy to punish those who misbehave.

You work in the House of Life, making medicines and filling prescriptions. For headaches you give sandalwood, and when people can't sleep, you give them poppy. Belladonna reduces fever, and garlic is a source of energy. According to the Ebers Papyrus, ancient Egyptian pharmacists knew how to make 700 different prescriptions. They even made cosmetics—not just so people would look good, but for health reasons. For instance, eye kohl was a real fashion statement (for women and men), but it also provided protection from the sun and from diseases carried by flies.

THE HOUSE OF LIFE
On temple property there was a building called the House of Life, where scribes, priests, and doctors were trained and where sacred scrolls were written and stored. Government documents were kept there too. Ordinary people came to the House of Life when they had a problem, were sick, or needed a dream interpreted.

PRESCRIPTIONS
Eye trouble and stomach problems were common complaints of ancient Egyptians. Here are remedies doctors might prescribe.
• For bad eyesight, pour a mixture of honey, red lead, and pig tears into the ear.
• For indigestion, put a crushed hog's tooth inside four sugar cakes. Eat one a day.

Doctor

Dentist

You are a priest who became a doctor by studying the medical paper in the House of Life. You spend your days helping sick people—rich sick people. Poor people can't afford to go to doctors. You know which gods rule over the different parts of the body, and you know how to call on them for their special magic. You treat wounds and mend broken bones. You are an expert in anatomy (the structure of the body), and you use sharp obsidian (hard, volcanic rock) tools to amputate limbs. Sometimes you prescribe medicine for your patients, and sometimes you send them away with charms and magic spells.

You might serve your corvée with the army, where you seal flesh wounds using a hot knife and then smear them with a mixture of honey and salt to keep the wounds from getting infected.

You are a doctor who specializes in teeth. Most of your patients are rich. They come to you with toothaches, gum disease, loose teeth, and bad breath. The most common problem is teeth that are worn down from years of eating bread containing sand and grit from the stones used to grind the wheat. Sometimes you tie a loose tooth to the one beside it so that it doesn't fall out, or you might drill a hole in a patient's jaw to drain an abscessed tooth. Other than that, you don't do dental surgery. Mostly you write prescriptions and chant magic spells to chase away the evil in people's mouths.

EBERS PAPYRUS

The Ebers Papyrus was a scroll—20 metres long!—with writing on both sides. It contained a lot of information about ancient Egyptian medicine. The Ebers Papyrus, along with the Edwin Smith Papyrus and other books of notes were important sources of medical information. Doctors had to learn all the information in these scrolls before they could treat patients.

CHAPTER 10

Artisan Jobs

Ancient Egyptians liked beautiful things. Pots, plates, jewelry, chariots, furniture, clothing, temples, tombs—it didn't matter—everything had to appeal to the eye. Things had to work too, of course, and this is where the artisans came in. (Artisan is a fancy word for craftsperson, and in ancient Egypt there were a lot of them.)

Each artisan was skilled in a particular craft and often worked in workshops with other artisans who did the same craft. These workshops would be connected to a noble's estate or even to a temple. Masters of the craft would oversee the artisans' work to make sure it was done properly. The best artisans worked for Pharaoh. Sometimes artisans could drum up enough business to set up their own shop—usually at home.

Paper Maker

Without paper makers, there would be no written records to tell modern people about ancient Egypt. So this is an important job.

Making paper isn't easy. You start by peeling away the outer skin of the papyrus plant and soaking the inner part in water. When it is soft, you cut it into strips, which you lay side by side. You put another layer of strips on top, making sure to run the strips the opposite way. Now comes the fun part. You hammer the layers together until they are one flat mushy mass. Then you put something heavy on top (to keep the wet paper flat) and dry the sheet in the sun. To get out any rough spots, you rub the finished paper with stones or pieces of wood. To make a scroll, you simply glue pieces of paper together.

Basket Maker

Sculptor

When ancient Egyptians went shopping, they didn't put their purchases in plastic or paper bags; they carried them in baskets balanced on their heads. Baskets were used to store things at home too. In fact, the first coffins were actually just big baskets with lids.

You make baskets from bulrushes, palm leaves, papyrus, and marsh grasses. Sometimes you make a framework of strong stems and weave the leaves or rushes around them. Other times you wrap bundles of plant fibers tightly together and sew them to make a coiled basket. To make the baskets beautiful, you braid in colorful geometric designs.

You don't just make baskets though. You also make rope from halfa grass and sleeping mats from papyrus stems.

Because sculptures were created to honor the gods, most of them were placed in temples. Pharaoh decided what statue he wanted, and the sculptor sculpted it. But just like painters, sculptors had to follow certain rules. It wasn't important for statues to look real; what mattered was that they looked powerful. Greek statues of the time showed action, but Egyptian statues were stiff and still and very serious-looking.

You carve your sculptures from stone. Sometimes a stonemason cuts a stone the size you ask for and you do the rest, but sometimes you carve a statue right out of a gigantic boulder. You may work alone, but because most statues are huge, you often work with other sculptors. It took a whole gang of sculptors to carve the Great Sphinx of Giza.

To begin a statue, a grid is drawn on rock— just as the monument painters do—to ensure the statue will be in proportion. Then the shape to be carved is laid out on the grid. A master sculptor is always on hand to oversee your work. He might even sculpt key parts himself.

You use a variety of bronze chisels, and tap carefully with your hammer. One wrong hit and your statue could have a split personality! For the finer work you use a pick. To smooth the finished statue, you rub it with stones and a gritty paste.

Woodworker

Potter

You are a woodworker—a carpenter. You build chairs, tables, wooden statues, board games, toys, musical instruments, and chests. Oh, yes—and beds—but just for rich people. Most Egyptians sleep on mats on the floor. You even make wooden headrests—people use those instead of pillows. Your bestsellers are canopic jars to store the organs of mummies.

The biggest challenge you have is finding wood to work with. There isn't a lot of that around, and you often have to join pieces together to get the lengths you need. When you build furniture you must keep it light, so that soldiers and merchants can carry it when they travel. You use your many tools well. You use axes, drills, and adzes for the big jobs. You use saws, mallets, chisels, lathes, and cane benders for the finer work. Finished pieces are painted and carved. Furniture made for wealthy Egyptians is often inlaid with gold and ivory.

Like all artisans, you put in long, hard days and are exhausted when you fall onto your mat each night.

Ancient Egyptian farmers treasured the Nile's rich, black soil. Potters treasured its mud. That was what they made their pots from. But not just pots. Potters were expert at making every kind of container you can think of.

If you are a potter, you can expect to get pretty dirty. This is a job you have to jump into feet first—literally! Before you can work the clay, you break up the lumps with your feet. This is called puddling. When the lumps are gone, you are ready to turn the clay into pots. You might mold the clay by hand, or you might use a potter's wheel. Unlike modern potters' wheels that are operated by a foot pedal, yours must be turned by hand. That means you have only one hand to make the pot, and that can get tricky. But you know what you're doing, and you quickly shape the clay. Then you leave the pot to dry. After that, it is time to decorate the outside. You might use a knife or sharp stick to engrave a pattern or carve a picture. Or you might rub the surface with pebbles to make it shiny. Next you put the pot in a really hot kiln (oven). This makes the clay resistant to water and turns it a reddish brown. You paint the finished pot to make it even more beautiful.

Jeweler

Metalworker

Ancient Egyptians wore a lot of jewelry. They wore two or three rings on each finger, and almost everyone had pierced ears—even the men—so there were a lot of earrings too. Amulets were popular too since Egyptians believed they protected the wearer against evil and illness.

Jewelry was made from shells, stone, faience (fy-ans) (a type of blue ceramic), and even bone. The metal bits were usually crafted from a mixture of gold and silver called electrum. Rich people's jewelry included gems such as amethysts, turquoise, and lapis lazuli. Poorer people wore ceramic beads.

Only men are jewelers. It is painstaking work. You are hunched over your workbench all day long. Unlike modern jewelers, you don't have a magnifying glass, tweezers, or other delicate tools to help you with this fine work. To make holes in beads, you must set them in plaster to hold them steady before you can use your bow drill.

Silver, gold, and gems are expensive, so you probably work in a workshop on a noble's estate.

When copper and silver arrive from the mines, your first task is to separate the metal from the rock. You do this by putting the rock chunks into a big pot and heating them over a fire. You use a bellows to make the fire scorching hot. You sweat from the intense heat, and your hands become rough and calloused from handling the rock. You don't smell very good either. When the metal melts, you pour it off, and throw away the rock waste, or slag. This process is called smelting. Sometimes you heat copper and tin together to make bronze. Or you might combine silver and gold to make electrum. This is probably done in one of Pharaoh's metal workshops, since all gold belongs to the king.

When the smelting is done, the molten metal is ready to be turned into tools, weapons, sculpture, and jewelry. You pour it into molds, weigh it, drill it, hammer it, scrape it, and polish it. Then you are done.

Only 999 more gems to drill for Pharaoh's necklace.

Glass Maker

AMULETS

Amulets are good luck charms. Most Egyptians carried at least one with them at all times. Here are a few kinds they might have worn:

The Eye of Horus looked like—well, the eye of the god, Horus! This amulet was supposed to keep the wearer from getting hurt or sick.

The Ankh (angk) is a hieroglyphic symbol that stands for life. Even the gods carried this amulet.

The Scarab looked like a beetle. It was a symbol of new life and life after death. This amulet was buried with a dead person.

Ancient Egyptians didn't use glass for windows—but they did use it for containers and jewelry.

To make glass, they mixed sand, lime, and washing soda and heated it in a hot clay furnace until the mixture melted. After it cooled and hardened, it was crushed and colored. Then it was heated until it liquified again.

To make jars and bottles, you pack clay around a long rod in the shape of the desired container. Then you dip it into the liquid glass to coat the clay. After that, it goes into a medium-hot oven so that the glass doesn't crack as it sets. When the glass object is cool, the clay mold inside is broken and dumped out.

Sometimes the molten glass is poured into long cylinders. When the glass rods harden, you send them to workshops where other glass artisans cut and polish them into beads or carve them into ornaments.

Does this sound like a job you could do?

CHAPTER 11

Daily Bread—and Beer—Jobs

Compared to ancient Egyptians, many modern-day people have an easy life. If you want something to eat, you go to the kitchen and grab an orange or an apple. It doesn't matter if it's winter and apples and oranges don't grow where you live in the winter. Maybe they don't even grow there in the summer. You don't think about that; you just enjoy the fruit. And if your parents come home from work and don't feel like cooking, you order in, and half an hour later supper is delivered to your door.

But in ancient Egypt, life wasn't that easy. For one thing, there wasn't as much variety. If a food didn't come from Egypt, most Egyptians didn't have it because only the very wealthy could afford imported food. There weren't any fridges and freezers to keep food from spoiling either. The only way Egyptians could preserve their food was to dry or salt it. Most food had to be made fresh every day.

The two main foods were bread and beer. Poor people—and there were a lot of them—made their own, but wealthy people had bakers and brewers make their bread and beer for them.

Grinding Girl

Baker

Before Egyptians could make bread, they had to grind the wheat and barley into flour. This is your job. You are a grinding girl. You put the grain onto a curved slab of rock. This is called a saddle-quern, because it is shaped a bit like a saddle. Then you take another rock and roll it back and forth over the grain to grind the wheat. Bits of blowing sand and rock chips from the grinding stones get mixed in with the grain, making the flour gritty. This makes the bread gritty too and wears down people's teeth when they eat it.

This job can be done by men or women. You bake cakes, pastries, and bread—mostly bread. Because Egypt is so hot, you work outdoors. You mix flour, salt, yeast, and water to make a dough. Then you add sesame seeds, honey, herbs, or fruit to flavor it. You know how to make over 50 kinds of bread. You shape the dough and set it inside a small clay oven that sits on hot embers. Egyptians eat bread at every meal, so it is not hard to find buyers.

Brewer

Cook/Chef

You probably work for someone rich. Like all Egyptians, nobles ate a lot of bread and beer, but they had much more variety in their diet than poor people did. They ate a lot of fruit, vegetables, fish, cheese, goose, duck, and sometimes meat. Rich people enjoyed hunting, so things like ostrich, gazelle, and ibex were special treats. As a chef you need to know how to prepare all these foods.

You use a mortar and pestle to grind up herbs and spices, and you use a sieve to strain things. Your kitchen is located behind the house or on the roof, because it's too hot to work indoors. Your employer has a lot of parties, so you often have to cook for many people. You boil vegetables, stew meat, grill fish, and roast fowl. You serve the food in pottery bowls and on plates. You don't need to worry about knives and forks, though, because Egyptians eat with their fingers.

Everyone in ancient Egypt ate bread and drank beer—even the children. But Egyptian beer wasn't very alcoholic, so that was okay. Beer was actually made of bread. Dried barley was baked into loaves of bread, which were then broken up and put in a large jug along with some dry grain. The mixture was then covered with water and left to ferment (turn into beer). Honey or dates were added for sweetness. The beer was ready to drink in about five days.

Egyptian beer was pretty lumpy, and the surface was covered with scum and insects that had fallen in. Gross! But don't worry. People drank the beer through a wooden straw with a strainer attached to trap all that stuff.

So, would you like to be a brewer?

Personal Appearance Jobs

Looking good was important to ancient Egyptians. It didn't matter if people were rich or poor, they had to be clean and presentable. Bathing was a daily affair, and clothes were laundered regularly. No one wanted to smell bad, so Egyptians used lots of perfumes and breath fresheners. They even had deodorant and toothpaste.

Both men and women used black eye kohl, and women carried their box of cosmetics with them wherever they went. Skin creams protected people from the sun and kept them from getting wrinkles. Egyptians colored their hair when it started to go gray—or they wore wigs. And everyone wore jewelry.

Most people's clothes were made of linen, though there was a big difference in the quality. Poorer Egyptians wore simple shifts and kilts made of roughly woven fabric. The clothes of wealthier Egyptians were made of the finest cloth in many styles and colors.

Tattoo Artist

Tattooing wasn't as popular in ancient Egypt as it is now. If you are a tattoo artist, you work in the streets. You use sharp, flat needles of bronze to inject the blue and black color (probably soot) into the skin.

Most tattoos seemed to belong to women. Some had collections of dots tattooed on their stomachs. Some had the god, Bes, tattooed on their thighs. Since Bes was the god protector of women and children, and since many women and babies died in childbirth, some experts think these tattoos were meant to protect pregnant women and their babies from harm. Still other experts think that Egyptians considered tattoos vulgar because it was mostly dancers and prostitutes who had them.

Barber

Manicurist/ Chiropodist

You are a successful barber in Memphis. You travel the city each day, doing people's hair right in the streets—a sidelock for a young man, braids for a woman, a ponytail for a little girl. People line up for your services. Shaved heads are very popular, because they are cool, clean, and keep lice away. Besides, who needs hair when there are so many attractive wigs?

In the afternoon you visit the home of nobles who are getting ready to go to a banquet. You wash and scent the noblewoman's hair, weave charms into it, and attach beautiful extensions using knots and beeswax. She admires your handiwork in a shiny, metal mirror. Then it is the nobleman's turn. You shave his head and face, then fit him with a handsome curled wig of human hair—after you take the bugs out of it, of course. He is pleased and pays you well.

Finally it is time to gather your barbering tools and go home. After a meal of bread, meat, and beer, you spend the evening sharpening your bronze razors, because tomorrow you must go to the Great Temple of Ptah to shave the priests.

You spend your days beautifying the hands and feet of wealthy Egyptians. You might not think that's such a great job—after all, who wants to deal with bunions, calluses, and athlete's foot? But people admire you because you get to work closely with nobles and royalty—maybe even Pharaoh himself. Other Egyptians kiss Pharaoh's feet, but you get to clip the toenails on them. You probably massage his feet too. Nail polish is very popular among your clients; it has to be red to show they are important people in society.

Like most other Egyptians, you must perform an annual corvée for Pharaoh. There's a rumor going around that this year you may be tending the feet of soldiers in Pharaoh's army.

Sandal Maker

Spinner

Making sandals is men's work. For regular Egyptians—the ones who can afford your services—you fashion sandals from papyrus reeds and leaves. Priests and priestesses wear papyrus sandals too. Wealthy Egyptians wear brightly colored leather sandals with turned-up toes. The sandals might even have cloth lining and be trimmed with gold. During wartime, army officers paint pictures of their enemies on the bottom of their sandals so they can grind them into the dirt. This is quite the insult.

Sandals aren't always worn outdoors. Mostly people walk around in bare feet, carrying their sandals in their hands. When they get where they're going, they wipe off their feet, put on their sandals, and go inside.

You and the other women in the spinning workshop turn flax plants into linen thread. You also spin the fleece from sheep into wool, but there's not much of a market for that. People think wool is dirty, not to mention itchy, so it's mostly used for outer garments like cloaks.

The first step in spinning is to shred the flax. You do this with large wooden combs. As the flax seeds fall to the floor, children gather them up. Some of the seeds will be planted to grow more flax, while the rest will be turned into linseed oil.

After the flax is combed, you roll the shredded fibers into balls and then carefully pull out a few strands at a time, twist them to make a thread, and wind the thread onto wooden rods.

Weaver

Tailor

Peasants usually made their own clothes, but wealthy Egyptians relied on the services of a tailor. Naturally they wanted clothes that made them look their best. Lucky for you styles didn't change much in 3,000 years.

Most men wear linen kilts. Female servants wear simple shifts. Noblewomen wear long dresses. Throw in a few loincloths, capes, skirts, and shirts, and that's it for Egyptian clothing. How tough is that! Clothes are usually draped, which means you don't even need to do a lot of sewing. A belt or sash here, a jeweled collar there, and everything comes together. Some garments are dyed, but you still can't go wrong with white. Add a leather belt and a snappy pair of sandals, and your customers are ready for the red carpet.

Weaving is a grueling job. There are 20 of you working in the hot, stuffy workshop. It is hard to breathe. What a relief when the door is opened and fresh air comes in. Sometimes you would like to stay home, but if you miss even a single day, the overseer will beat you. Every weaver in the shop has a different job depending on what each person does best. The looms are laid out on the floor, so you must work on your hands and knees, feeding the linen thread through and pushing it tight. Wealthy people expect fine, gauzy fabric. Sometimes the finished linen is dyed in bright patterns; other times it is embroidered with gold thread. But it is always beautiful.

Wig Maker

In ancient Egypt, both men and women wore wigs. Children wore them too. It was easy to tell people's place in society by the type of wigs they wore. The cheapest ones were made from plant fibers. Mid-quality wigs were a combination of plant fiber, sheep's wool, and human hair. The most expensive wigs were made completely of human hair. Only the richest Egyptians could afford to wear those. People who couldn't afford wigs had to settle for having extensions braided into their hair. Of course, if you were bald, that could be a bit of a problem.

Ancient Egyptians tended to own many wigs, even though they wore them only on special occasions. The rest of the time they were stored in special wig boxes.

When making a wig, you start with a piece of shaped net and weave the hair or plant fiber into it. Then you style the wig. If it is a short-haired wig, you curl the hair in rows. You design the wig so that the forehead of the wearer will partly show, but the ears and back of the neck are completely covered. Long-haired wigs are made so that the hair hangs from the top of the head to the shoulders. You pad the wig with palm fiber to make it fuller. Sometimes you put a wave in the hair, and sometimes you twist or braid it. For the very wealthy, you even slide gold tubes over the plaited hair for decoration. You scent your wigs with flower petals or cinnamon chips.

CHAPTER 13

At-Your-Service Jobs

Some ancient Egyptian jobs are hard to label. They weren't linked to Egypt's geography. They weren't done to create a product. They didn't require any special skills. But these jobs were still an important part of ancient Egypt.

Steward

Slave

If you are a steward you run a noble's estate. You don't actually do the cleaning, cooking, farming, weaving, or mucking out of the animal pens. Your job is to supervise the people who do that work. You are also responsible for purchasing things for the estate and for keeping the household accounts. Since you have to provide your master with accurate records, you must be able to read, write, and do math.

Like the other servants, you live on the estate away from the main house, but because your job carries more responsibility, your quarters are bigger.

In ancient Egypt there weren't many slaves— mainly just foreigners who had been captured in war or Egyptian citizens who sold themselves to get out of debt. Masters could sell or rent out their slaves, but they were not allowed to mistreat them. Even though slaves weren't free, they had rights. They could marry whom they wanted and they could own property. When an owner died, slaves were often given their free- dom. Though some slaves were sent to work in the quarries and mines, none worked on the pyramids. Most worked at domestic jobs. They were brewers and bakers, gardeners, maids, child minders, and stablehands. Some even learned trades. If a slave was trustworthy and learned to read and write, he might even be promoted to steward of his master's estate.

Lodge Keeper

Gardener

Temple grounds and noble estates were private property. They were surrounded by tall, thick walls that kept unwanted people out. As the lodge keeper, it is your job to guard the gate in the wall. You decide who goes in and who doesn't. If Pharaoh comes to visit, let him in.

If you are a gardener, it is your job to take care of the flowers, trees, and other plants at the temples or on the estates of nobles. These gardens often surround large pools or ponds, which are stocked with fish and have papyrus plants and lotus flowers growing in them. You keep these pools clean so that they attract birds.

Because Egypt is so hot, shady spots are a must. Trees do the trick nicely. The most popular ones are tamarisk, acacia, and willow. Sometimes you plant date and fig trees too. These provide shade *and* fruit. You can also create shady arbors by winding grapevines around tall columns. Between the trees you plant poppies, daisies, and cornflowers—pomegranates too. These plants not only smell good and make the garden beautiful, but they can be used to decorate the homes of nobles when they hold a party. Flowers are also a popular offering to the gods.

If you are going to be successful at your job, you must know how to irrigate the land and keep plants reproducing. If you have a green thumb, you might make a good gardener.

Welcome!

Servant

Policeman

Because there were laws in ancient Egypt, there were also police to enforce them. But instead of arresting people, Egyptian police usually punished lawbreakers right on the spot. For instance, if a man tried to cheat on his taxes, the police would make him lie on the ground and then beat him with a big stick. In the cities, police patrolled the streets, ready to pounce on lawbreakers. In rural areas, they protected farmers and herders from thieves. Police also roamed the edge of the desert with trained dogs, looking for robbers and escaped prisoners.

If you are policeman, you might work at a tomb construction site. You protect the workers, but you also protect the tomb. You check it each day to make sure it is intact, and at night you stand outside to discourage anyone who might think about robbing it.

Servants worked on big estates for wealthy Egyptians. Many servants cleaned the house, cooked the food, and waited on the nobles. Others looked after the grounds, animals, and outbuildings. Both men and women could be servants. Being a servant was an honest, respectable job—even if it didn't pay very well.

Indoor servants swept the floors and kept the house free of rats, flies, fleas, lizards, and other pests. An onion stuffed into a snake hole and cat grease smeared around a mouse hole both worked very well. Servants fetched clean water and disposed of dirty water—usually by throwing it into the street. They also served food at parties, and when the eating was done, they went around with jugs of water that they poured over the guests' sticky fingers.

Some servants were personal attendants to the nobles. They helped them bathe, dress, do their hair and apply their makeup. Personal servants also gave massages and accompanied the lady of the house when she went out in public.

Midwife

Wet Nurse

A midwife is a woman who delivers babies.

When you are called to assist with a birth, you move the mother-to-be to the roof of the house or to a shady place in the garden. This area is called the confinement pavilion. The mother and baby will stay here for 14 days. This allows them to have a good rest and protects them from infection—a good idea, since many babies die in infancy.

During delivery, the expectant mother squats on the ground with her feet on bricks decorated with hieroglyphs. You crouch in front, ready to catch the baby as it is born. Other women stand beside the pregnant woman, holding her hands and encouraging her. Sometimes you place a bowl of hot water under the pregnant woman, so the warm steam will speed things up. After the baby is born, you care for the mother and baby until they are ready to leave the confinement pavilion.

There was no formula or baby bottles in ancient Egypt, so all infants were breastfed. If a mother couldn't nurse her baby, another woman—who had recently had a baby—did it for her. This woman was called a wet nurse. Becoming a wet nurse to a noblewoman's baby was one of the few ways ancient Egyptian women could climb the social ladder. Not too high though. Wet nurses to royal babies had to be married to high-ranking government officials.

If you are a wet nurse, you have probably signed a contract agreeing to nurse only the noblewoman's baby and your own. You agree to do this for three years. You also agree to live in the nobles' house and have no more children while you are nursing. You care for the baby when it is sick. Your employer provides you with food and pays you well—often with necklaces, combs, and cooking oil. Wet nurses were well respected and were often asked to stay on as nannies to the children they had nursed. In fact their relationship with the family often lasted a lifetime. Royal wet nurses were granted special privileges and tombs.

CHAPTER 14

Entertainment Jobs

Ancient Egyptians worked hard, but they liked to play too. They enjoyed swimming and sailing, having picnics, playing board games, going to parties, and attending religious festivals. They also liked athletics. They were especially fond of poetry, music, and dancing. A party wouldn't be complete without singers and dancers on hand to entertain the guests.

We know about Egyptian poetry through the hieroglyphic writings the ancient Egyptians left. The musical instruments they played have been found in tombs. Paintings show us how they danced. But we can only guess at what their music sounded like, because ancient Egyptians didn't have sheet music, MP3 players, or CDs.

Dancer

Musician

Though most dancers in ancient Egypt were women, there were male dancers too. But men and women didn't dance together. Dancers were hired to perform at religious ceremonies, festivals, banquets, and funerals. The dances they performed were carefully planned out, and many of the movements were done in unison. Some dances told a story and looked like ballet. Others were quite acrobatic with cartwheels and backbends all over the place. Dancers didn't wear a lot of clothes. In fact, sometimes they only thing they had on was a loincloth. A dance troupe might be independent, or it might be connected to a temple or to the harem of a nobleman.

Have you got rhythm? You might want to be a dancer.

You are a temple musician. You and the other musicians in your group perform at religious ceremonies, funerals, and festivals. All the instruments—the flute, lyre, trumpet, cymbals, sistrum, and bells—create a beautiful sound. Dancers and singers perform as you play. Sometimes you visit farms at harvest time and play while the workers are bringing in the crop. Temple musicians are much admired, and as a harp player you are especially respected. Musicians of royal households enjoy a respected status too. However, professional musicians who hire themselves out to play at private parties are a step or two down the social ladder.

Songstress

Wrestler

Singing was a big part of life in ancient Egypt. Farmers sang while working in their fields. Herders sang to their cattle. Professional singers performed at parties and banquets while musicians played and the audience clapped in rhythm.

You are a noblewoman and priestess at the Temple of Isis. You are also one of the temple songstresses. Accompanied by a harp, you sing hymns in honor of the goddess during religious ceremonies. Sometimes—performing with priests—you sing to honor male gods too. You sing songs honoring the dead as well.

You hold an admired and respected position in Egyptian society.

Ancient Egyptians were big sports fans. They enjoyed boxing, rowing, high jump, tug-of-war, archery, and gymnastics as well as many other sports. Probably their favorite was wrestling. Wrestling competitions were regular events, and a nobleman hosting a banquet might entertain his guests by arranging a whole evening of wrestling matches. Referees were on hand to make sure the competitors wrestled by the rules.

Adolescent boys were encouraged to wrestle too. Adults thought it would toughen them up. During a wrestling game, a group of boys would gang up on one of their friends. The cornered boy had to try to escape any way he could. If he succeeded, he was a hero. If he didn't, he was sore and bruised.

CHAPTER 15

Tomb Jobs

Because the afterlife was so important to ancient Egyptians, getting ready for it was a big deal. There was the body to prepare and the coffin to make. Then, of course, there was the funeral to plan and the tomb to build and furnish. There were also mourners to hire and a funeral barge to reserve. So dying was big business, and a lot of Egyptians earned a living from it.

Embalmer

Everybody knows that ancient Egyptians made mummies. But did you know they didn't do it on purpose—at least not in the beginning? It just happened when they buried people in the desert. You see, the desert was very dry and it contained salt and natron, which kept bodies from deteriorating. It didn't take Egyptians long to figure this out, and after that, all they had to do was improve on what nature was already doing.

You are an embalmer. You are a doctor-priest who mummifies bodies. Because embalming is a religious process, you wear a mask of the god Anubis (the god of embalming) while you work. Egyptians have mixed feelings about what you do. Though most choose to be embalmed when they die, they think it is morally wrong to cut into a body. *Continued on page 90*

Embalming can take up to 70 days. You work in a special tent. First you remove the body's internal organs, except for the heart. Egyptians believe the heart is the source of a person's intelligence, so it is left in the body. However, you pull the brain out through the nose with a hook. Next you cover the body with natron and drain the fluids by placing the body head down on a tilted table. You leave the body to dry for 35 to 40 days. Then you fill it with spices and clean linen. The spices help preserve the body and make it smell good; the linen keeps it from caving in now that it has nothing in it. Once that is done, you rub the body with oils and lotions to soften the skin. You apply a layer of sticky plant juice called resin to make it waterproof. Now you wrap the body in linen bandages—up to 20 layers! Finally you decorate it with jewelry and a wig, and place it in its mummy case.

Cutter

You work for a famous embalmer. It is your job to make an incision in the body being mummified, so that the lungs, liver, stomach, and intestines can be removed.

The good thing about being a cutter is that there isn't much competition for your job. Most cutters are criminals or people who can't find other work. The bad thing about being a cutter is that many people don't approve of what you do. They think cutting a dead person is wrong. So they sometimes curse you or chase after you with stones. A cutter needs to be a fast runner.

CANOPIC JARS

Ancient Egyptians believed that people needed their internal organs in order to be reborn in the afterlife. So the lungs, liver, stomach, and intestines were removed during the embalming process and packed in natron salt to preserve them. Then the organs were wrapped in linen strips and put back inside the body or stored in containers called canopic jars that would be buried with the mummy.

Mummy Mask Maker

Mummy Case Maker

Before a mummy was wrapped in linen bandages, a mummy mask was made. Masks were usually made of cartonnage—a kind of papyrus papier-mâché that was glued together with resin.

If a person was royalty, you might make a mask of gold. You might even decorate it with beautiful jewels. Once you shape the mask, you paint it to look like the dead person. The finished mask is placed on the mummy after it is wrapped in its linen bandages. This helps the person's *ba*, or soul, recognize itself in the afterlife.

Could you be a mask maker?

After a body has been embalmed, it goes into a mummy case. This is made of old papyrus and plaster called cartonnage. While the cartonnage is wet, you mold it to the body's shape. When it hardens, it forms a shell around the dead person. You paint a face on it, as well as colorful scenes and hieroglyphic messages to help the mummy on its journey into the next life.

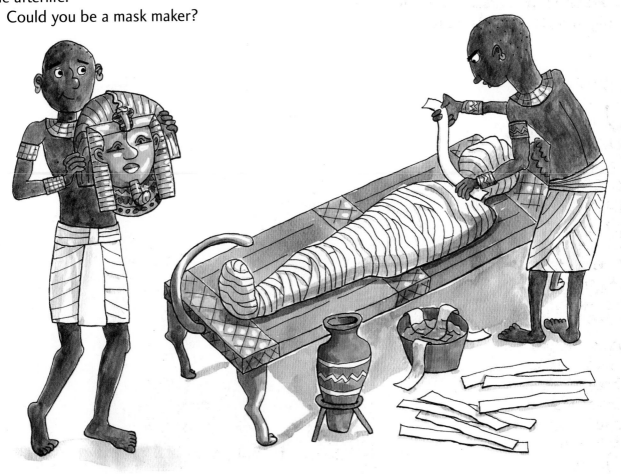

Coffin Maker

Sometimes, instead of—or as well as—a mummy case, the body went into a coffin—or two—or three. Royalty often used several coffins that fit one inside the other. Some coffins were metal or ceramic, but most were made of wood—mainly cedar. A coffin could be a rectangular box with a removable lid, or it might take on the shape of the body inside. The richer the client, the more extravagant the coffin. Some were even inlaid with gold and jewels.

No matter how fancy or plain coffins were, they had to provide the dead people inside with the things they would need for the challenging journey into the afterlife. Coffins were decorated with pictures of events the dead people were expected to experience. Gods were painted on the coffins too, along with the dead person's promises of loyalty. Magic spells and prayers were written all over the coffin, and offerings to the gods were tucked into the coffin beside the mummy. A few amulets were thrown in too. Mummies needed all the help they could get.

SHABTIS

When ancient Egyptians died, they looked forward to being reborn in the next life and living as they always had—except for one thing. They didn't want to do any work, so they had little statues of people buried with them. These figurines were called *shabtis*, and they were supposed to do any tasks the dead person might be called upon to perform in the afterlife.

VALLEY OF THE KINGS

Only a small number of pharaohs had a final resting place in pyramids. Many more were buried in huge tombs carved into desert cliffs. These tombs were easier to hide than pyramids and therefore safer from robbers. A Pharaoh's funeral was a grand affair. Egyptians stood on the banks of the Nile watching an ornately decorated barge carry the king's body from the capital city of Thebes across the river to its final resting place in the Valley of the Kings.

Sarcophagus Maker

Mourner

You might think that linen bandages, a mummy case, and several coffins was plenty of protection for any mummy—royalty or not—but there was still one more container for the mummy to go into. That was the sarcophagus.

You make the sarcophagus from stone and carve pictures and hieroglyphs inside and out. Most sarcophagi are box-shaped.

The most famous sarcophagus belonged to King Tut. It was made of yellow quartzite and contained three gold coffins.

You are a professional mourner. This is a woman's job. You are hired to grieve for someone who has died. It doesn't matter if you knew the person or not. Having hired mourners means the dead person had been rich, and so everyone is impressed.

Being a mourner isn't just a one-day job; it lasts from the time the person dies, right up to the burial—around 70 days. You spend your days outside the embalmer's tent while the body is being mummified, and on the day of the funeral you accompany the mummy to the tomb. That's a long time to be moaning and wailing, beating your chest, and banging your head. For special effect you throw dust in your hair and on your clothes too.

If you cry easily and enjoy causing a scene, you might like being a mourner.

OPENING OF THE MOUTH

The dead person has been embalmed, has a death mask, a mummy case, a coffin, a sarcophagus, good luck charms and spells, and a tomb filled with food and objects to make life in the next world comfortable. It is time to begin the journey. There is just one more thing to do. When the funeral procession reaches the tomb, the mummy's coffin is placed upright and opened. A priest wearing the head of Anubis holds the mummy so it doesn't fall out. Two other priests touch the mummy's mouth, eyes, and ears with a wand. This is called the Opening of the Mouth and is supposed to give the dead person the ability to breathe, see, hear, speak, and eat. In other words, Opening the Mouth brings the mummy back to life.

RECOMMENDED FURTHER READING

To find out more about life in ancient Egypt, see the following books.

Aubin, Henry T. *Rise of the Golden Cobra.* Toronto: Annick Press, 2007. Red Maple Award Finalist 2008

Set in 728 BC, this story surrounds the reign of Pharaoh Piankhy, the brilliant and compassionate leader whose astonishing campaign united ancient Egypt. Bursting with action, political intrigue, and military strategy in enticing historical detail, and peppered with dramatic illustrations, *Rise of the Golden Cobra* is an epic adventure for the ages.

Cline, Eric H. and Jill Rubalcaba. *The Ancient Egyptian World.* New York: Oxford University Press, USA, 2005.

Taking readers back 4,000 years, to the fertile land around the Nile River, *The Ancient Egyptian World* tells the stories of the kings, queens, pharaohs, gods, tomb builders, and ordinary citizens who lived there. Using papyri, scarabs, tomb inscriptions, mummies, and a rich variety of other primary sources, Eric H. Cline and Jill Rubalcaba uncover the fascinating history of ancient Egypt.

Greason, Susan. *Death of a Princess.* Sydney: Little Hare Books, 2005.

A story for history and mystery lovers, this novel is set in ancient Egypt in the palace harem of Ramses II. When Pharaoh's eleven-year-old daughter dies suspiciously, Meryt, the harem's beautician, is suspected of killing her. Can she find the real murderer before it's too late? Ages 10 – 14.

McGraw, Eloise. *The Golden Goblet.* New York: Puffin Books, 1986. Newbery Honour Book

Orphaned Ranofer wants nothing more than to be a skilled goldsmith like his father. But circumstances are working against him. Abused by his older brother, Gebu, he finds daily living a struggle in itself. But when Ranofer discovers a golden goblet bearing an inscription to the pharaoh, Thutmose, he suspects Gebu is more than just evil—he may, in fact, be a grave robber. Proving it without getting himself killed is another matter. Ages 9 – 12.

McGraw, Eloise. *Mara, Daughter of the Nile.* New York: Puffin Books, 1985.

Because of her facility with languages, Mara is elevated from slave girl to spy. Working for Queen Hatshepsut in the palace at Thebes, she is charged with reporting the activities of Thutmose III—the rightful heir to the throne—to the queen. Things become more complicated and dangerous when Mara falls in love with Sheftu, a loyal noble of Thutmose, and ends up spying for him as well. If she should be found out by either side, she will be killed. Ages 9 – 12.

Rubalcaba, Jill. *A Place in the Sun.* New York: Scholastic, 1998.

It was just an accident. But when Senmut's sculpting chisel slips from his fingers, striking and killing a dove, Egyptian priests exile the nine-year-old to a lifetime of hard labor in the gold mines of Nubia. Jill Rubalcaba evokes the vast, exotic world of thirteenth century BCE Egypt during the reign of Ramses II in this scorchingly suspenseful novel about a boy who dares to challenge the seemingly indestructible bonds that tie him to his fate.

ACKNOWLEDGMENTS

It has taken the combined efforts of a multitude of people to make this book happen. There were the ancient Egyptians, of course, whose amazing 3,000-year civilization inspired the book in the first place. Then there was Annick Press, who offered me the opportunity to write it. Thankfully Priscilla Galloway and Laurie Coulter penned the previous books in the series, establishing the general format and tone, and providing me with excellent examples to aspire to. Research was a challenge. Since much of what we know about ancient Egypt is derived from artifacts and hieroglyphic documents and wall drawings, findings are somewhat open to interpretation, and the books and Internet resources I used occasionally contradicted one another. Having Egyptologist Dr. Lyn Green check the book for accuracy was a huge help. Once she had verified (and corrected) what I had written, it was time for Martha Newbigging to bring the text to life with her fun illustrations. For me to describe the term *sidelock* would have taken a lot of words, but with a few strokes of her magic pencil, Martha managed the job perfectly.

We writers tend to get so absorbed in what we are working on that we are often unable to see the flaws. That's where editors come in. Many thanks to my editor, Carolyn Kennedy, for gently showing me the error of my ways and for making suggestions that definitely improved the book. Thanks also to copy editor Nancy Christoffer, who made sure the final text was clean and polished and art director Sheryl Shapiro, for the fantastic book design. Finally I would like to acknowledge Sandra Booth for keeping us all on task and Brigitte Waisberg and her marketing department for launching the book into the world. I know there are many more people who had a hand in this project, and though I don't know who you are, your contribution is much appreciated.

INDEX